CAN I HAVE YOUR YOUR *Pearl* *Bracelet?*

CAN I HAVE YOUR
YOUR

Pearl Bracelet?

Frances H. Kakugawa

WATERMARK
PUBLISHING

© 2023 Frances H. Kakugawa

ISBN: 978-1-958701-07-2

Library of Congress Control Number: 2023944297

Design and production by Dawn Sakamoto Paiva
Author's photo by Jason Kimura
Front cover photo: iStock.com/Mari Franz

Watermark Publishing
1000 Bishop Street, Suite 806
Honolulu, Hawai'i 96813
Telephone (toll-free): 1-866-900-BOOK
Website: www.bookshawaii.net

Printed in the United States of America

This book is dedicated to you

OTHER BOOKS BY FRANCES H. KAKUGAWA

FOR CAREGIVERS

Mosaic Moon: Caregiving Through Poetry

Breaking the Silence: A Caregiver's Voice

I Am Somebody:
Bringing Dignity and Compassion to Alzheimer's Caregiving

CHILDREN'S BOOKS

Wordsworth the Poet

Wordsworth Dances the Waltz

Wordsworth! Stop the Bulldozer!

Wordsworth, It's In Your Pocket!

Wordsworth the Haiku Teacher

MEMOIRS

Teacher, You Look Like a Horse!
Lessons from the Classroom

Kapoho: Memoir of a Modern Pompeii

Echoes of Kapoho

POETRY

Sand Grains

White Ginger Blossom

Golden Spike

The Path of Butterflies

Dangerous Woman

Contents

Introduction

Gwen Lee and I sat around her dinner table, our hysterical laughter filling the house as we talked about my final book. To Gwen's, "What's your next book going to be?" I replied, "I'm going to write about when I get Alzheimer's. The title will be *Did I Tell You I Have Alzheimer's?*"

Gwen added, "All the chapters should be titled 'Did I Tell You I Have Alzheimer's?'"

We began to say, repeating, "Yes, and every chapter will begin with "Did I Tell You I Have Alzheimer's?'"

We laughed because I was far from losing my cognitive skills, at least in both our minds. I had cared for my mother who had Alzheimer's, and this gave us both permission to bring humor to the disease. I had even written a poem for my future book:

I Am

I remember when my heart first got broken.
I took my pen and ice-picked that grief
Into a zillion frozen pieces
Until there was nothing left but my poetry.
When that grief got published, I rejoiced and said,

"Grief is good."
I threw myself against arrows, fearless, soared
　　beyond clouds, unafraid.
"This is a poet's life!" I said.
Life became a cardiograph of mountain tops and
　　craters
Distanced from that staccato beep.
Life was all mine. Grief all my own.
"I am a poet!" I said
Until they stamped Alzheimer's
On my chart. There is no ice pick
Sharp enough to chip away my amyloid plaque.
I'm still a poet, I said.
I am a poet... I said. I said.
I said, "Did I tell you?"

Then the pandemic hit. What do you do during a pandemic that never ends? It's been more than three years, a lifetime behind bars. The months kept turning into a new year, and with each year, another birthday, and with each birthday, thoughts of my own mortality. "You'll live to be ninety-five," the physician predicted, but are doctors seers? I look at the obituaries and notice the deceased are closer to my own age than ever before.

It was a time for reflection. My youthful outhouse literature in the Hawaiian village of Kapoho, the *Reader's Digest*, with its jokes and Most Unforgettable Character stories, came to mind.

Why not use my pandemic time to preserve what I can of those unforgettable characters who made a difference or more precisely, made me different? So here they are, my own *Reader's Digest* stories of memorable characters, including two stories titled "Frances the Fraud," snuck in behind my back by a little mouse poet. Some of the names have been changed, and a number of the stories, revised for this book, have appeared in other publications. The final book will have to wait.

These stories were written to honor those who made a difference in my life, those who helped me become the person I aspired to be. Sometimes the best teachers are found not in classrooms but in the most ordinary places, such as a book or a restaurant or a hospital, or even in a place called Kapoho. I hope these stories will make a difference in your life, dear reader, for why are we here if not to help each other and future generations become more humane, more compassionate and more ourselves? Isn't this who we are meant to be, for as Dr. Lydate said in George Eliot's *Middlemarch*, "What do we live for if not to make the world less difficult for each other?"

—Frances H. Kakugawa

Dead Poets Alive

Dear William Wordsworth,

I was a lonely child growing up in Kapoho, always wanting more than what was there, so I escaped into books but that didn't seem to help as the novels weren't even an inch closer to life in Kapoho. My parents weren't like those in novels, no one conversed with me as fathers and mothers did with their daughters. We didn't even have a car to take family vacations to faraway places. There were no Christmas carolers at our door with snowflakes dancing down from the skies. Our plantation house was no house on the prairie. Then one day, there you were with your poem, "I Wandered Lonely as a Cloud." Suddenly I was you, wandering in your vacant and pensive mood, and I have never stopped walking with you.

I wandered lonely as a cloud
That floats on high o'er vales and hills,
When all at once I saw a crowd,
A host, of golden daffodils;
Beside the lake, beneath the trees,
Fluttering and dancing in the breeze.
Continuous as the stars that shine
And twinkle on the milky way,

They stretched in never-ending line
Along the margin of a bay:
Ten thousand saw I at a glance,
Tossing their heads in sprightly dance.
The waves beside them danced; but they
Out-did the sparkling waves in glee:
A poet could not but be gay,
In such a jocund company:
I gazed—and gazed—but little thought
What wealth the show to me had brought:
For oft, when on my couch I lie
In vacant or in pensive mood,
They flash upon that inward eye
Which is the bliss of solitude;
And then my heart with pleasure fills,
And dances with the daffodils

—"I Wandered Lonely as a Cloud"
by William Wordsworth

You opened my heart to the beauty and restorative power of nature. I still find daffodils in unexpected places and remember them long after they are gone. I even named a poetic mouse character in my children's books after you. Ah, William Wordsworth, I owe you so much. So did Senator Ted Kennedy, whose favorite poet was you, so at his funeral service, President Obama recited lines from your poem "Character of the Happy Warrior:"

As tempted more, more able to endure.
As more exposed to suffering and distress,
hence also more alive to tenderness.

My Dear Elizabeth Barrett Browning.

You awakened in me, even before I was ready, what it meant to be loved. I envisioned throughout my youth that someday I would love as deeply as you and somewhere in the future, a Robert Browning will be waiting for me, too.

How do I love thee? Let me count the ways.
  I love thee to the depth and breadth and height
  My soul can reach, when feeling out of sight
  For the ends of being and ideal grace.
  I love thee to the level of every day's
  Most quiet need, by sun and candle-light.
  I love thee freely, as men strive for right.
  I love thee purely, as they turn from praise.
  I love thee with the passion put to use
  In my old griefs, and with my childhood's faith.
  I love thee with a love I seemed to lose
  With my lost saints. I love thee with the breath,
  Smiles, tears, of all my life; and, if God choose,
  I shall but love thee better after death.

—"How Do I Love Thee?" (Sonnet 43)
by Elizabeth Barrett Browning

I stood up for you once, before an old poetry professor, and I even walked out of his class for good. On the first day of class, he asked us for our favorite poet and after a freshman student said, "Elizabeth Barrett Browning," that pompous professor smirked and laughed. "Bah," he said, "This is why you're here, to know what good poetry is. Who reads Elizabeth Barrett Browning!"

My hair was not the only part of me that stood on end. I also stood and knew I could be expelled from his class, losing three credits, but the passion your poetry had awakened in me overcame whatever consequences lay ahead.

"How can you ridicule her for her choice? I was in high school when Elizabeth Barrett Browning's poetry came to mean so much to me. Don't we pass through different stages in life, taking the poetry we love along with us? Don't poems that speak to us lead us to explore other poetry, some of which you may consider good or better? Can't you allow us this... to develop our own taste in poetry as we grow and experience what life brings us? Weren't you once as young as that student, Professor?"

The professor was dumbfounded that I had defied him. He was speechless and almost choked; I thought he was having a stroke. The other students applauded my words, but he abruptly ended his class and dismissed us. I never returned to his class, refusing to allow him to give me F for the course. Now that I am older, I wished I had stayed. Thank you, Elizabeth, for never leaving me.

Dear William Cullen Bryant,

I was going through a strange period in eighth grade when I found you. An awareness of my own mortality began to fill my nights with fear. I even had a dream about my own funeral, looking down at my own coffin. In the dream, I had died being hit by a passing car, which would have been unusual since there were very few cars in Kapoho. I lay in bed at night, afraid of dying in my sleep. Perhaps that "Now I Lay Me Down to Sleep" prayer we learned in elementary school had taken root in my subconscious mind, especially the frightening ending, "If I should die before I wake," and middle school provided fertile ground for my fear to sprout. Then one day the teacher introduced your "Thanatopsis," and I saw images of myself lying next to all the great dead kings and emperors. "Hey," I thought, "after death, I will not be alone. Dying can't be that bad."

> Yet not to thy eternal resting place
> Shalt thou retire alone, nor couldst thou wish
> Couch more magnificent. Thou shalt lie down
> With patriarchs of the infant world—with kings,
> The powerful of the earth—the wise, the good,
> Fair forms, and hoary seers of ages past,
> All in one mighty sepulcher.

—"Thanatopsis"
by William Cullen Bryant

I memorized the following last stanza and it became my mantra. Today, in the last decade of my life, I trust I will not go scoured, but sustained and soothed... for I have lived fully and passionately.

> *So live, that when thy summons comes to join*
> *The innumerable caravan, which moves*
> *To that mysterious realm, where each shall take*
> *His chamber in the silent halls of death,*
> *Thou go not, like the quarry-slave at night,*
> *Scourged to his dungeon, but, sustained and soothed*
> *By an unfaltering trust, approach thy grave,*
> *Like one who wraps the drapery of his couch*
> *About him, and lies down to pleasant dreams.*

> — "Thanatopsis"
> by William Cullen Bryant

Dear Sylvia Plath and Dylan Thomas,

You taught me to use expletives! Yay! You gave me freedom to curse and express all my suppressed passion in poetry. I was raised under that "nice girls don't swear" and "what will others think" roof. How I yearned to free myself from the constraints of my upbringing, that feeling of being trapped like an insect in a spider's web. Then there you both were, with your bold, outspoken poems, and slowly that web began to lose its sticky hold on me. Sylvia, your "bastard," and Dylan, your passion, began to set me free.

Sylvia, how courageous and liberated to be able to say this to your father:

> *There's a stake in your fat black heart*
> *And the villagers never liked you.*
> *They are dancing and stamping on you.*
> *They always* knew *it was you.*
> *Daddy, daddy, you bastard, I'm through.*

—"Daddy"
by Sylvia Plath

If you can write "bastard," why, my use of "damn" is mild in comparison, and the ink began to flow freely from my pen. I even used "bastard" in a poem in this book's epilogue!

And Dylan, you taught me to rage against the dying of the light. To not live in neutral but to live unafraid and free.

> *And you, my father, there on the sad height,*
> *Curse, bless, me now with your fierce tears, I pray.*
> *Do not go gentle into that good night.*
> *Rage, rage against the dying of the light.*

—"Do not go gentle into that good night"
by Dylan Thomas

I developed a great schoolgirl crush on you, Dylan, wishing we could have gone to a pub together and discussed life and love over a pint. I wanted all of you, and I was frustrated that all I could have was your poetry. But that was enough: your rage awakened mine and still fuels me to this day. Settling with your poetry left a feeling of want. But that rage became inborn and what a life, Dylan. To remember the impact you made on my life, one of my characters in my children's book series is named Dylan.

3 A.M.

As the world
Empties into sleep
I wonder why
For some of us
It's mountain tops
And valley greens,
Sky-bound jets
And subway trains.
Never in between.

—from *Dangerous Woman*

Each step a footprint, yet
Had I feared backward glances,
I would have been nowhere
Nowhere at all…

—from *Dangerous Woman*

Years ago, at a tea hosted by university professors' wives, I was invited to read some of my poetry. After seeing all the well-dressed women in white gloves, I was unsure about reading a poem that included the word "damn." When I asked the other guest poet what she thought about it, she looked at me and replied, "I have *fuck* in one of my poems." Well, that was permission enough for me, since I already had Sylvia's and Dylan's! So I read the following poem that day, with all the expletives and passion I learned from you both:

Overcooked Peas from Eyes of the Young

A man and a woman quietly sit,
Her gray in a bun, his hair in a bald.
They show no bond except for a ring
Proclaiming vows between the two.
They use their eyes on overcooked peas,
They touch their legs against Lysoled chairs.
Their lips only move to meet each spoon.
They sit and eat, a man and his woman.
Damn you, woman,
How can you sit
Concentrating on peas?
How can you not share
Your thoughts over his?
How can you not feel
His pulses beat?
How can you waste
The presence of him?
Damn you, woman, look at his eyes,
Damn you, man, don't look at your peas.

Tell her your sighs, your woes, your dreams,
How can you sit and look at your peas?
Where is that touch, that look, that feel
That once had formed that golden ring?
Damn you both, for dying so young.
Damn you both, for looking at peas.

I encountered many more brave and defiant poets as
I matured, but you were all my very first. And like first
loves, you will always live in my heart.

Dead Poets Alive

It was the dead who kept me alive
Those years growing up
Confined in a village so isolated,
The only communication by way of
An unpaved road without family cars,
A battery-run radio,
Three party line telephones.
It was the dead who took me beyond
Catalogs of Sears and Montgomery Ward,
Dream-makers of that remote village
On the day I discovered an oracle
Within the pages of poets long gone,
Promising a wondrous world
For the me, alive, but not yet formed.
Memorizing lines from "Thanatopsis,"
Reciting Poe's "Annabel Lee,"
Aching with "How Do I Love Thee?"
Dreaming in isolation

In the attic with Emily Dickinson.
Yes, Yes, I said.
Believing in Sara Teasdale's
"Life has loveliness to sell,"
I was impatient to meet those roads
Knowing I could not travel both.
I fantasized sinking a thousand ships
To becoming a phantom in delight,
And rage, rage against the dying of the night.
Damning those whose pain I wore.
Yes.
The dead gave me dreams
Of the woman I would become
Long before I became.
But oh, how "I wandered
Lonely as a cloud."

The Waste Basket

Emi was a sixth-grade student who never raised her hand in class, whispered her conversations with me and shyly nodded or shook her head in response. Her face blushed red with embarrassment. After recess one day, a group of boys stood around her desk teasing her. Suddenly her voice rang out: "Fuck off!" The words filled the classroom floor to ceiling with stunned silence. All heads turned toward me. The boys hurriedly walked backwards to their desks, their eyes on me. I motioned to Emi, and she followed me outside. Trembling with fear, her face was flushed like a dark pink paint brush across a canvas.

I knew that fear. I once shook with that same fear in a high school classroom.

That was not an ordinary day, like today. The state superintendent was paying a visit to our school. We were all on alert with the campus cleared of all litter and students told to be on their best behavior. The word of the day was, "Don't make any trouble."

I was caught committing the worst of crimes, chewing gum in class.

"Is that gum in your mouth?" the Social Studies teacher shouted. "Spit it out right this minute!"

I slowly took my gum, aimed it at the wastebasket near the door and tossed it like a basketball free throw. It arced through the air just as the principal and the superintendent came to the door. My gum fell on the principal's black leather shoe. My face lit up in panic when I realized I could be suspended for my unpardonable act. I knew about suspensions, having already received one in fifth grade for writing a nasty note about my teacher.

The principal, in a suit, instead of his usual aloha shirt, motioned me to him. I walked toward him, a sheep to the slaughter. Without a word, he pointed at my gum wad on his shoe and then at the wastebasket. I grabbed the gum and scurried like a frightened mouse to toss it into the wastebasket. He nodded with a little twinkle in his eyes and he and the superintendent turned and left the room. During this encounter, the teacher kept on teaching and no one knew of my exchange with the principal.

Emi was trembling before me now and there was no wastebasket for her to throw the word "fuck" into.

She looked up at me as I slowly said, "Emi, that must have felt soooo good." The panic drained from her face, she wrapped her arms around me and began to cry. I let her cry herself out and whispered, "Go to the bathroom now, and come back when you're ready." Emi returned to the classroom a little later, traces of tears still on her face. The class was silent. I could almost hear them:

"The teacher must have really given it to her." The word lingered around for the rest of the day, looking for a wastebasket. For me, it was the day I became the kind of teacher my principal had taught me to be so long ago.

A Tin Man's Tears

The second grader was one of those children whose soul seems to be in his eyes, like Margaret Keane's painted eyes. It wasn't only Brian's eyes that bore into mine with intensity but the lack of patches of hair on his head that made me feel my own inadequacy during my once-a-week visit as a writing resource teacher. For his sake, I wished there was something I could do, some God-given power to change what I knew could not be changed.

Brian listened intently to the poems I read in class. His eyes never left my face. His poems were filled with thoughts and feelings uncommon for a boy his age. He wasn't unique in that way. There was Nicky, a sixth grader from class who was able to use poetry to find her way.

Nicky had had her leg amputated because of cancer and she wasn't able to let any one of us forget that. Her attitude, "I have cancer, you know, so I need special attention," confused her classmates, who knew she needed empathy, yet her constant reminders created social distances among her peers. It was through poetry that she finally found her way to deal with her cancer after we had the following conversation:

She: Why didn't you choose my poems to be recited at the State Curriculum Fair?

Me: Why don't you write more poems?

Her poems were all about butterflies and rainbows, so I continued with, "Write more."

She: Why are you still rejecting my poems?

Me: Nicky, these aren't good enough. Why don't you write about things that are very close to your heart? Something that you think about a lot when you're alone and have deep feelings for?

She looked directly at me and said, "You mean like my cancer?"

I replied, "If that's what you feel deeply about, yes."

She wrote the following poem in less than fifteen minutes. She went to the Curriculum Fair and recited "Life" flawlessly.

Life

Before I could run
Through the big white fields.
Before I could skip like a stone over water.
Before I could hang on the bars
Like all the other girls.
Before I could play dodge ball
And climb a banyan tree.
Then the doctor came in

With a strict look on his face.
He said, "This is a horrible disgrace.
Next week on Tuesday, your leg will be gone.
The test shows cancer has come along."
My leg is now gone,
I feel lonely and sad.
Does God still love me?
Pain is what I have.
I'm going to succeed
Because I have hope.
I've discovered I can write
Of my feelings and my fears.
I'm glad I can let others know how I feel.
I'm glad I can read my poems,
It helps a great deal.
It's time to sing
Another song.

—from *Teacher, You Look Like a Horse,* edited

One day Brian asked me to read aloud a poem he'd written. The class applauded which brought a big smile on Brian's face.

Your Voice

I like your voice.
Your voice makes me feel
I am in church.
Your voice makes me feel safe.
I wait for your voice

Every Wednesday morning.
I like your voice.

I took his poem home with me, along with all the poems the students had written. I couldn't let go of the strong emotions hammering in me, nor could I sleep, until all was released in the following poem I wrote late into the night.

A Tin Man's Tears

The light from my fluorescent lamp
Magnifies the order of disarray across my desk.
I sit and stare, page after page of poetic lines,
Assignments written in class today.
A child's "I'm all poemed out"
Keeps beating repeatedly in my head
Like the surf against my thighs.
I sit, moved beyond any human emotion
To see their souls bared so nakedly
Before my eyes.
I turn off the light of my fluorescent lamp
Seeking refuge on my bed.
But the naked souls continue to stare down at me
From the darkened ceiling, walls.
My mind moves with the shadows
Cast by the street lamp
Through my translucent pane.
Oh, but to have a magic wand.
A magic wand to find a cure for cancer
That ravages his young, total being.

To take away that veil of confusion and fear
That occasionally sweeps across his face
And now across his page.
A magic wand to sober Jackie's father
So her eyes do not cloud the memory
Of what was the evening last.
Her poems shout of anger, whisper of sadness
Of how life ought to be.
Oh, to be God or the Wizard of Oz:
To take the tears refusing to fall
From David's eyes,
Frightened and confused as he goes through
    divorce
With his mom and dad. To bring that mischief
Back into his once laughing eyes
So he can once again write of bikes and soccer
Instead of fear of a motherless world.
To bottle cap that joy on Adam's face
As he writes of love and fun with such wit
They bring a chuckle to my throat.
And to desensitize Wendy
So she can see beauty without the sense of loss
From a poet's heart.
And for myself, limited,
A wizard's transformation
For this hour of my day.
To gather the sheets
For tomorrow's class.
I, not God, only a teacher
To hand each child a key to their poetry

As the Wizard of Oz
Gave each what was needed
And sent Dorothy home.

—from *Teacher, You Look Like a Horse*

The week before my last classroom visit, Brian followed me out of the classroom and said, "I had a dream last night. I was all grown up and you and I were having dinner by candlelight in a nice restaurant."

Brian did not survive his cancer treatments. Even so, he managed to grow up to be a young man in the short time he had, enjoying an imaginary dinner with a woman in a restaurant. I did not have to be a god to help him do that.

A tree was planted in his honor. I sat in the back at the ceremony, behind the other students, wearing my sunglasses, and a supply of Kleenex on my lap. The custodian had dug a hole on the side of the playground. I watched intently as Brian's father, in his soldier's uniform, lowered the tree into it.

He set the shovel down, turned to all of us and said, "Thank you for remembering my son with this tree. I want you to know that it's not guaranteed that this tree will grow into a large tree, even with your watering and care because sometimes, even with the best of care, the things we plant will not survive. And this is okay."

Cow 1 is not Cow 2

Under the rising sun
The enemy came
Wearing my face.
After Pearl Harbor, I became the enemy
After 9/11, the enemy was Islam.
After Covid-19, it was China.
Now the enemy wears Putin's face.
Putin brutalizes Ukraine
Your Russian neighbor looks like Putin,
Speaks Putin's language, but he is not Putin.
Cow 1 is not Cow 2.
My ancestors bombed Pearl Harbor,
I look like my ancestors.
Careful, careful, Cow 1 is not Cow 2.
Such a simple, uncomplicated rule.

Semanticist Dr. S.I. Hayakawa wrote "Cow 1 is not Cow 2" on the blackboard when I was a young college student in Hawaii. The class topic was how language and our perceptions often lead to racism. He explained: You are driving along the country road and you see a cow. Further down the road, you see another cow. That cow is not the first cow you saw. A black man robs you at gun point. The next black man you see is not the man who robbed you. An Asian rudely cuts in front of you at the cashier. All Asians are not that Asian who cut in front of you. Cow 1 is not Cow 2.

Another day he passed out his publication on general semantics, titled *ETC*.

"One evening," he began, "I was in a pretty pricey restaurant as a guest of friends. I watched a well-dressed man at a nearby table order a bottle of wine, steaks and dessert. Lucky waiter, I thought, he is getting a big tip tonight. After his leisurely dinner, the man left a paper bill on the table for a tip and went to the cashier to pay his tab, which I saw ring out to over $90. I assumed that tip probably was a one-hundred-dollar bill. Curious, I took a look. Son-of-a-gun, I thought. What a miser. He had left a dollar on the table.

"ETC: Our assumptions based on what we see may not be what it is. We don't know, do we? Etcetera, Etcetera, Etcetera."

He was a visiting professor at the University of Hawaii Summer Session when I took his six-week course. I knew his reputation as a semanticist and digested every word he uttered. His words became my truth. The day he described the difference between a Democrat and a Republican, I became a lifelong Democrat. Later, he would change parties and become the first and only Republican Japanese American Senator in Congress, representing California. His outspokenness and habit of dozing off in meetings and sessions that bored him drew criticism. He came to be known as Sleeping Sam.

Even the most adored idol's halo can tarnish.

I remained a Democrat.

I was an avid reader of the *Reader's Digest* in the outhouse in Kapoho, the village on the Big Island where I grew up, so my hair stood on end when Dr. Hayakawa commented that no intelligent student would cite the *Reader's Digest* in a research paper. "He's an intellectual snob," I thought. My defiant Kapoho child awakened. I cited *Reader's Digest* as one of my resources on my research paper on semantics. Hayakawa acknowledged my defiance and circled the citation in red. Then he gave me an A anyway.

It was a summer of dichotomy, a summer of yin and yang, of *War and Peace*, of Hayakawa and Edward Teller. Teller was the father of the hydrogen bomb and lecturing that summer as well. I listened to him propose that a nation can be best prepared for peace by having the world's most powerful weapons. I preferred Hayakawa's passionate belief in language and dialogue as the way to peace. It led me to wish he would run for President or be a delegate to the United Nations. And for Teller to zip his mouth.

Long after his retirement, I spotted Hayakawa at the Hilo Airport. It was Christmas Eve; he was walking toward the baggage claim area. He looked older and walked with a slight stoop. "That's Hayakawa! That's Hayakawa!" I thought.

He looked around, scanning the crowd of hurrying travelers, perhaps searching for his host. But no, he was looking for me! He must have read my thoughts. He walked directly toward me, and I jabbered like a schoolgirl: "Mr. Hayakawa, I was in your class in the sixties at UH Summer School. You were so wonderful." He took my outstretched hand and thanked me. He asked for my name and wished me well.

Walking toward his cab, suitcase in hand, he turned, searched the crowd again and told the cab driver to wait. He came back to me, nodded and said, "Have a happy holiday. Merry Christmas, Frances." I had been rather depressed that evening. A broken heart from a relationship. This kind man, who I hadn't seen in a long time, who was detested for his role in student-faculty strikes at San Francisco State University in 1968, and had cast me adrift from his politics, lifted my spirits that evening.

Dr. Hayakawa had been the interim president of San Francisco State University for less than a week when student radicals and faculty protested the Vietnam War and demanded the inclusion of Ethnic Studies in the curriculum. On live television, he was seen ripping wires off the protestors' loudspeaker, earning him the name "Samurai Sam." He broke the strike and restored normal classes, adding Ethnic Studies to the curriculum. I followed his career from across the Pacific and my personal contact with him in that summer class and now at the airport overrode all negative and sensational media press that followed him to Congress. A Canadian who became an American citizen, he angered the Japanese Americans by remaining cosmopolitan in his view about internment camps. Hero or villain, Dr. Hayakawa was always a hero in my eyes, because this man taught me, ETC. and Cow 1 is not Cow 2 and he wished me a Merry Christmas on a sad Christmas Eve.

The Winter Coat

She always caught cold after returning from a visit to see her Mother Superior on the East Coast. Why she traveled during winter in her thin Hawaiian wear, she didn't say. Sister Ruth, I will call her, lived with three other nuns in a cottage on Oahu.

After returning for two winters in a row with a bad cold, I told her, "Sister Ruth, we're going to get you a winter coat before your next trip. You can't come home with a cold every winter." Ignoring her claim, "I don't need a winter coat, I have enough sweaters," I drove her to the outlet in Pearl City. It was like watching myself at the mall. Her excitement and enthusiasm were a total delight. She tried on a few coats, giggling with joy, asking, "Are you sure? Oh, this is so beautiful." She settled on a full-length grey woolen coat with a matching scarf. The next winter she returned without a cold. The coat became the House Coat and whenever one of the nuns traveled to their New England abbey, it was the item of choice.

I come from a Buddhist family. A good friend of mine, a Catholic, introduced me to Sister Ruth and the other nuns. "You need to meet these nuns," he said. "They are so special, and they won't impose their religion on you. You will get caught up with the joy that they radiate."

He was right. Their ability to find joy in the simplest things, accompanied by an innocent playfulness that the nuns exhibited reminded me of another sister I had met in Honolulu while attending summer school at the University of Hawaii, Manoa. Over dinner one night, Sister Carol shared the following story with me. "I went to the beach in Waikiki today, and this sailor sat next to me. We had such fun talking. Since I no longer wear the traditional habit, he didn't know I'm a nun, and I believe he was flirting with me. I went along, knowing I could go to confession later. He said his ship was sailing the following day, but he would like to see me again after he returned. He asked for my phone number and promised to call me in three months. So I gave him Mother Superior's number. Imagine his surprise when Mother Superior answers the phone!"

One evening, I invited the four nuns to dinner in Waikiki. They oohed and aahed like children at the night lights, the festive décor and menu items, taking time to select their dinner; it seemed like Christmas all over again. I decided I would be in the company of four lady friends, not nuns. When I began by offering a drink, they all looked at Sister Ruth for approval. She said, "Well, when Father Keating was here recently, he enjoyed his glass of wine, so I don't see why you can't do the same. I'm sure Father Keating would approve." At the time, I didn't know Sister Ruth was struggling with liver problems; she was the only one who declined the wine that turned all of us into happy hens. After a round of drinks, Sister Ruth seemed to get some contact joy from the rest of us.

The nun stuff started to fade away. We were becoming a group of friends out on the town for a little fun. I went out on a limb and said, "How about going to a bar next time for a glass of wine?" The nuns all looked at Sister Ruth, hoping for a nod, but she said, "No, that is not a good idea," much to their disappointment.

I received a note from Sister Ruth thanking me for the dinner:

> *April 6, 2005*
>
> *Dear Frances,*
>
> *Thank you for your note. Yes, it was a fun night with you and my sisters, and yes, we must get together again. But not in a bar, dear Frances! Perhaps for coffee and/ or dessert?*
>
> *God bless you and keep you happy and at peace.*
>
> *Lovingly,*
> *Sister Ruth*

I visited them often with sinful desserts or fruits and vegetables. I told myself they could always go to confession. "Sister," I once joked, "I could have been a nun in my last life. When I was in Lourdes, France, I joined the nightly parade of people who walked with lighted candles toward the site of St. Bernadette's cave. Two nuns invited me to join them. I even took a sip of the holy water. Why would the nuns pick me out?" Sister shook her head as she often did to my stories.

Under the Vatican II reforms, these nuns practiced a less conservative form of Catholicism and were not so orthodox. Once, a Catholic friend confided to Sister Ruth that she needed to go to confession because she had not been to church for years. Sister told her, "Oh, go in your backyard, dig a hole and bury all your sins. That will be confession enough."

During this time, I experienced a bout of depression. I'd published a collection of poems written by members of my poetry-writing support group for caregivers in Honolulu. We all stipulated that all royalties would go to Alzheimer's research. When the book became a success, a few members claimed they were entitled to a portion of the royalties. Their claim went nowhere but the fact that they had become so selfish and turned a good intent into a legal contest weighed on me. The doctor suggested various medications, which I rejected. I'd seen what the side effects had done to a close friend. So I turned to Sister Ruth. Maybe her God could do the job.

Over lunch, I explained the cause of my depression. She shared some of her personal history and admitted she often experienced inner turmoil because her basic human needs for intimacy and affection were not being met. Just sharing these stories of disappointment helped me. My depression slowly lifted after our talk, though why it did still remains a mystery to me. The doctor was puzzled that I had gotten over the depression without medication or therapy. When he asked me how I had done it, I said, "I spent a whole day with a nun."

After I moved to California, I visited Sister Ruth each time I went home. On my last visit, her health was deteriorating. I sat next to her holding her hand, feeling sad to see her shrunken face peering out from between the sheets. The afghan I had given her a year before was on her bed. "Frances," she whispered, "Dying is not that easy. I keep asking God to take me home, but I am still here." God did call Sister Ruth home a few days later. I attended her funeral and met her family, who had flown in from the Midwest. After the service, her brother greeted me with a hug and said, "You must be my sister's friend, the one who bought her the winter coat."

Lessons from Micronesia

Before the plane landed in Micronesia on the atoll of Majuro, it circled four times close to the ground to chase the pigs off the tarmac. I was with a group of professors from the University of Hawaii Teachers College. We had a six-week summer contract to teach continuing educational courses to teachers, principals and administrators on the atoll. One of the professors told me an intriguing story of a nun named Sister Katherine who was born to a Micronesian woman and a Japanese soldier during WWII. This nun was active in the educational system of Majuro and would probably be a student in my summer course on literature and writing.

I didn't recognize her immediately. She had retired from the order and no longer wore a traditional nun's habit. Except for her Japanese last name, she was entirely Micronesian and showed no trace of her Japanese ancestry.

In 1980, Majuro was an atoll with very limited conveniences. Water hour happened twice a day, an hour of water in the morning and the other at night. I often had to resort to brushing my teeth with beer. Grocery stores were sparsely stocked with little but canned goods and soft drinks. Airplanes from Australia and Hawaii arrived every three weeks with supplies to replenish grocery shelves. The two restaurants served fresh fish, lobster and crabs from the surrounding sea. The Japanese restaurant served tofu and fish with miso which became my weekly dinner. The other restaurant had large nets hanging above the linen tablecloths, placed there to catch any rats that dropped from the ceiling. It wasn't unusual to hear that muffled thump of a falling rat while dining.

I was given one piece of advice upon arrival: *you can run over a child but never ever run over a pig; they are too valuable.* One day while driving a stick-shift rental car, I almost hit a child. A little boy at the roadside suddenly covered his eyes with both hands and, in a burst of laughter, ran in front of my car. Fortunately, the brakes were good! He must have thought that what he didn't see didn't exist.

A few weeks before arriving in Majuro, I was diagnosed with mitral valve prolapse. The cardiologist gave me a copy of the test results to take with me. On the first day of class I asked, "So what happens if one gets a heart attack here?"

Without hesitation the students replied in unison, "Oh, you die."

Katherine became my host. She invited me to her modest apartment and cooked Japanese dishes, rightly suspecting six weeks of canned goods and Cokes would kill me. Somehow, she managed to get fresh vegetables and fruits.

A year before our arrival, a severe storm had devastated the atoll. Katherine related how she'd run to the Catholic church, sat in the pews while the storm raged and waited to die.

The U.S. government sent thousands of disposable diapers as part of their relief aid. A year later, dirty diapers were still strewn across the atoll and clogging the water system. They were everywhere, along with hundreds of empty soda cans that littered the beaches and dotted the ocean.

I called the radio station and suggested a Clean Our Atoll Day. The American announcer advised against it. He explained, "Micronesians do not use the word *no*. If you asked them anything, they will say *yes* politely to not offend you and then they won't follow through." He was right.

Time seemed to mean nothing to Micronesians. I would remind my students daily that class began at 10:00 a.m., and would they please be prompt. They promised to be prompt and then would trickle into the classroom half an hour late. Finally, summoning up all the bluntness I could muster, I voiced my frustrations.

"This class begins at ten o'clock. I expect everyone to be here at ten. I want you to respect this. I know being on time is not so important in your culture. Here I am, among you in your culture, and I'm respecting your ways. We are seven degrees from the equator and it's hot. Why am I wearing long skirts down to my ankles in this heat? To respect your culture that frowns on women showing their knees. I would rather be wearing shorts, but out of respect for you, I don't. I ask that you do the same for me because in my culture, we are on time."

For the next few days, I found notes on my desk, child-like notes. "Please, please forgive me, I am so sorry, I will never be late again." Katherine, my Micronesian cultural advisor, laughed and said, "Frances, do you realize one of the men in your class is a delegate to the United Nations?" She laughed again, "And he asked for your forgiveness for being tardy? He is very highly regarded here in Micronesia. You must be the first person to scold him. You should be a diplomat! You'd be a sensation in the Diplomatic Corps!"

The students were a delight to teach. They fell in love with *Charlotte's Web* and the little spider's world. Their own stories and poems were filled with lovely imagery drawn from their own natural world of the atolls. The majority of them expressed sentiments of hope and love. One student, though, wrote chillingly about the atomic bomb testing on Bikini, replete with metaphors using Jesus Christ and an evil eagle to stand in for America. Another, Jeo, wrote a poem about his young son choking to death after playing with a piece of cord. "Forgive me, Jeo, I wrote him, "for putting the poet's pen in your hand, I know you still grieve for the son you lost. I hope writing it down helps to comfort you a little."

The first summer, we compiled our stories and poems in a booklet titled *The Wave of Micronesia*. Each student received a copy. The second and third summers' writing were also collected as *The Second Wave of Micronesia* and *The Third Wave of Micronesia*, including illustrations done by the students as well.

Seemingly child-like in some ways, or unforgivably tardy to class, Micronesians can also be prone to take whatever is said to them in its most direct and literal meaning. A principal in class told me this story: A Christian minister had taken a Micronesian high school student back with him to the States to continue his education. The boy happened to be a superb athlete as well and was offered a football scholarship. When he played his first game, the coach told him to go *break a leg*. During the game, the boy grabbed an opponent's leg and fractured it. All the newspapers characterized him as *that uncivilized savage* until an enterprising reporter dug a little deeper and was able to explain the misunderstanding.

Near the end of my third summer, the university professors on Majuro were dropping like flies with Hepatitis A. An hour before departure for home, I took a drink at the bar and immediately I felt my body burn with heat. That flight home was the most uncomfortable I have ever taken, and afterward I was diagnosed with Hepatitis A.

Katherine and I became close friends and confidants over time. I felt comfortable in asking her questions that would have seemed inappropriate earlier. For example: How do nuns take showers if a woman's body is not to be exposed?

"We took group showers with our breasts bandaged tightly with yards of cloth. It was sinful to expose our breasts, as the Mother Superior would be quick to remind us if we did. We also wore a thin robe to cover the rest of our bodies."

Katherine was a rebel, like Maria in *The Sound of Music*, and was often punished before leaving her order. She had once questioned Mother Superior's nightly outing to meet a male friend, and Katherine was punished the following evening at dinner. She was told to sit at the end of the rectangular table. A plate with a boiled head of a rooster, complete with feathers, red wattle and comb, was passed from nun to nun to Katherine. Each nun looked at the rooster's head and silently passed it on until it came to Katherine. Katherine looked at the rooster's head, looked at Mother Superior at the other end of the table who nodded at her to begin her dinner. Katherine stood and walked out. The next day, she left without her habit.

Katherine reminded me of my own journey, a long series of forks in the road, the ones being less traveled. Getting an education was the first fork that both of us came to. I took mine by trying to get rid of my Hawaiian

Pidgin that the University of Hawaii frowned upon and working as a live-in maid to pay for my room and board.

Katherine got on the road to her education by writing letters to all the large corporations in America, asking for financial aid to continue her education in the U.S. "I want to be educated in America," she wrote. "I know a full scholarship is impossible, so I would appreciate whatever financial aid you offer." The checks dribbled in, in small amounts, a few hundred here, a few hundred there from companies like Coca Cola, Chevron, General Electric and others. She finally had enough to escape her limited surroundings and to finance her Bachelor's and Master's degrees at American universities.

Not all roads less traveled are without bumps. Katherine's parentage was a source of unresolved inner turmoil. She resented her father's family in Japan, assuming they were living an affluent life while she and her mother had to survive on next to nothing during and after the war. "Someday," she said, "I want to face that family of his. I want them to hear my story."

Katherine taught me much about going through or around the obstacles on the paths of getting to where I wanted to be. There was one road she had not traveled that I wanted to offer. Katherine was still living the life of a nun under her street clothes. "Katherine," I asked her one day, "before you die, don't you want to know what it is like to experience a man?"

"I know nothing about men. Where do I begin? I haven't even been on a date."

By then, the six-week summer course was over. I had returned to Hawaii, but my mentorship was not over. How was I to help her feel comfortable about her own sexuality and realize that a sexual life was not sinful? From a distance, all I had were novels. I'm not sure if I sent her *Lady Chatterly's Lover* or *Fannie*, but I did send her other novels with explicit "how to" bedroom scenes between loving couples. A colleague who knew what I was doing warned me to be careful or I might create a monster I couldn't control. I laughed him off.

The following summer when I returned for another six weeks, Katherine was there to greet me at the motel. She was wearing a spaghetti-strap dress, her long black hair loose over her bare shoulders. OMG, I thought, what have I done? Not only did she now feel free to express her sexuality, but she had returned to Japan to meet her biological father's other children.

She described her visit as we shared a pot of tea. "I entered my half brother's house," she began, "and was met by his family. I walked directly to the family shrine. I saw a framed photo of my father. I offered incense. His Japanese children sat behind me. We didn't speak. After offering incense, I turned and they bowed to me and I returned their bows. I then turned back to the shrine to look at the other framed pictures. I saw a faded photo of my mother. It was then my tears began to flow. We didn't speak much because of our language barrier. I went to Japan with anger, but returned with acceptance and love."

She was not dating yet, had not found anyone of interest, at least no one to match those romantic men in the novels I had sent.

Then I received a bombshell of a letter after my final summer in Majuro. She wrote, "I'm getting married. I want to thank you for giving me this new life. I met an Australian pilot who flies supplies to the atoll. He is now in Australia, and I am going to Australia to be married there. I will be passing through Hawaii, will you be able to meet me at the airport?"

I met her with a pair of crystal champagne glasses, cash for a bottle of Australian champagne and a lacy white shawl. I kept my doubts to myself and bade her a good life. I had seen that pilot at the bar, a handsome, robust, blond man enjoying drinks and laughter with the local men. She wrote once, married to her pilot. She was enjoying freedom she could only dream of had she remained a nun. She will land on her feet, just as she had taught me, those summers on an atoll where life's simplest things, like rain drops, a children's book or water hour, brought the greatest joy.

Mrs. Honda's Beautiful Daughter

When Mrs. Honda died, one of my two faces was buried with her. It's a mystery how messages are received in small plantation villages where there are no private telephones, local newsletters, or community bulletin boards. In Kapoho, a village of less than a thousand people, the following message from the plantation hospital was delivered to every household where a five-year-old lived: *All children entering first grade should have their tonsils removed by Dr. McKenzie.*

Even at five years of age, I was suspicious of the hospital and Dr. McKenzie. They called him "Horse Doctor." No matter what the symptoms, when villagers went to his office, they walked out with the same pills. Soon they would share them with other family members. It saved more trips to the hospital.

"Horse Doctor" or not, he was the only doctor available, unless my parents borrowed someone's car to drive us to a private doctor in Hilo. Even so, city doctors were viewed with some suspicion. And, Horse Doctor was cheaper.

When my ten-year-old sister complained of a severe stomachache, my parents decided this was too serious for the plantation doctor and took her to Hilo. Within minutes the physician made his diagnosis: "It's her appendix; it needs to come out today."

My mother thanked him and hurried my sister out of the office and took her to Mrs. Maeda, the village midwife and witch doctor. Mrs. Maeda was there when my mother's water broke and my brother was coming out feet first. Mrs. Maeda had magic in her hands; little massage, and my brother turned, and came out headfirst. That's why my mother took my sister to Mrs. Maeda that day.

"No, no," Mrs. Maeda said, after pressing my sister's stomach, "No need for surgery. *Yaito* will fix this." She marked a spot on my sister's arm and instructed, "Burn six yaito three times a day on this spot until pain is gone."

Yaito was a simple remedy, though extremely painful. Mugwort herbs called *moxa*, aged and ground into a fluff like lint from a dryer, were a staple in most Japanese medicine cabinets. My mother placed a pearl-sized fluff of moxa on the spot marked on my sister's arm and lit it. A tiny flame engulfed the moxa and burned itself out. She repeated this as instructed. My sister did not even whimper. After all, being burned was better than having someone cut your stomach open. She had no problem with her appendix after the yaito treatment, though she still bears a burn scar to this day at ninety.

For cuts and bruises and other ailments, we would go to our neighbor Nalani for her native Hawaiian medicine. For diarrhea, we chewed the young leaves of the guava plant and swallowed the bitter juice. For cuts and scrapes, we chewed the young guava shoots, applied them to the open wound to stop the bleeding. Squatting over the steam of burning fig leaves cured hemorrhoids and a piece of aloe worked as well as a suppository.

One day, my father fell off the roof and lost consciousness for a few minutes. Nalani gave him a cup of warm water mixed with Hawaiian sea salt. He recovered completely.

But when the message about tonsillectomies buzzed around the village, we all paid attention. "Horse Doctor" or not, Dr. McKenzie was still the voice of medical authority, so I was on his waiting list with other five-year-olds in Kapoho.

Mrs. Honda, one of the mothers in the village, placed even greater faith in doctors, or anyone with a title before their name. She scheduled her daughter, Hiroko, to be the first to have her tonsils out that summer. News of Hiroko's surgery traveled rapidly. There would be no other tonsillectomy that year. Hiroko died on the operating table. The Horse Doctor had overdosed her with ether. I still have my tonsils today.

The villagers, dressed in black suits and dresses showed up for Hiroko's funeral service at the Honda home. Hiroko's casket was surrounded by orchids and azaleas from people's yards. The scent of incense and the soft Buddhist sutra from the priest greeted me when I entered the room with my mother. Imitating my mother, I went up to the Buddhist shrine next to the casket, lit a stick of incense and placed it upright in the incense urn with all the others. I put my hands together in prayer and followed my mother to Mrs. Honda.

Mrs. Honda was weeping, "What shall I do? What shall I do?" to everyone who offered their condolences. No one had an answer. Hiroko was her youngest child. Hiroko was irreplaceable. Mrs. Honda was inconsolable.

When it was my turn, Mrs. Honda reached out and touched my face. "Hiroko, Hiroko, *honto ni kawai*," truly precious, so beautiful. Before I could say anything, someone pulled on my skirt and hurried me along. But they were too late. In that brief moment, I became two daughters.

A few months later, I passed Mrs. Honda on the way to the store. She stared at me, and then began to weep and said, "If Hiroko were alive, she would look like you." I stared back at her without saying a word.

During my teens, whenever we met, Mrs. Honda would look at my face and say, "What a beautiful face. Hiroko would look exactly like you." Those years, I looked like a photo on a care package, in loosely fitted homemade dresses and a haircut styled by my father's scissors. Mrs. Honda never noticed. She'd say, "Just look at your flawless complexion." She was mercifully blind to my freckles and pimples, my small "single-eyes" and skinny body.

My family teased me each time I ran home bragging, "I saw Mrs. Honda and she said I was beautiful."

"Yeah," my brother Paul laughed, "Just like a morning glory, all dried up at the end of the day." To this day, Paul still calls me MG.

Mrs. Honda worked as a laborer in the cane fields. Whenever I saw her in her work clothes, with a towel covering half her face to protect it from the sun, she was full of apologies and embarrassed to have me see her in her oversized, long-sleeved denim shirt, her pants tied at the waist with a cord. On her feet, were a pair of denim Japanese *tabi* with rubber soles.

"Look at me in these work clothes," she'd say. "Look at my face, so dark and ugly. But look at you. Your face is so beautiful. Hiroko would look like you today."

I accepted her compliments with a smile. Mrs. Honda had just outshouted the boys in the hallway, the same boys who hid *Playboy* under their mattresses, the ones who whispered, "Eh, Stew Bones" as I passed by, clutching my over-sized jacket over my chest.

To have discounted this compliment, even from a naive and simple woman, would have denied Mrs. Honda her image of Hiroko, and Stew Bones the confidence to take off her jacket. I wonder if Mrs. Honda knew what a lift she gave me that day.

Mrs. Honda also extended her family by one other member: my father. He occasionally worked with Mr.

Honda on the papaya farm after his retirement from the sugar plantation. One day, he returned home from work saying, "That silly woman. Today she packed a lunch for me, too."

"Ohhh," I teased, "She has a crush on you."

We all knew Mrs. Honda checked the work schedule and on days when Mr. Honda and my father worked together, she would pack fancy lunches with food usually reserved for New Year's Day: sushi, shrimp tempura and *nishime.*

"Look at that *bakatare* woman," Mr. Honda would say, "I don't know what got into her," and then he'd spread her lunch for the two of them. Mr. Honda allowed Mrs. Honda these simple pleasures, chalking them up to his wife's continuing grief.

Whenever I saw Mrs. Honda going past our house with her head down, I'd call out to my father, "Come quick. Come quick. Your girlfriend is passing." I could tell Mrs. Honda didn't want to be noticed in her dirty work clothes.

My father would chuckle, "You can say whatever you like."

When my father died, Mrs. Honda was the first to arrive to offer her condolences. She openly wept and called out my father's name. I was older then and held her to me. We hugged each other as if we'd always been doing that.

A few weeks before my high school graduation, my photo appeared in the *Hilo Tribune Herald* for a scholarship that I had received. The next day, Mrs. Honda stopped me on the roadside and said, "If Hiroko were alive, she'd be just like you. Smart and beautiful."

In Mrs. Honda's eyes, Hiroko had accompanied me to college, and we both became teachers. After graduating from college, I didn't see much of her, but when I did, she would always say, "Hiroko would have become a teacher just like you."

On one occasion she said, "How lucky you have a tall nose, just like a *haole*. Look at your white complexion, just like a haole. You are truly beautiful." I was a college graduate, a grown woman, but still I had the urge to return home to tell the family, "Mrs. Honda still thinks I'm beautiful."

When my first four books were published, Mrs. Honda attended each of my book signings. Though she was *issei* like my grandmothers, and never learned to read or write in Japanese or English, she bought my books, held them in both hands and bowed.

Why she chose me among all the girls in the village, I will never know. But, to Mrs. Honda, the child who became her surrogate daughter was the most beautiful child in Kapoho. Her face glowed with love and affection when she looked at me, and I accepted her praises with a smile.

When Hiroko died, there were whispers in the village that it could have been a blessing. "She would have struggled in school," they said. They did not believe that Hiroko could ever become an independent adult or meet someone someday who would have accepted her as his wife. Children teased Hiroko. They called her "Mochi-Face," as they once called me "Stew Bones."

My face has now turned into a wadi bed, and my skin is mottled with dark liver spots, and my hair, sparse and white. I want to hear Mrs. Honda saying once more, "Hideko-san, you are beautiful."

The Eastern Road

The old Buddhist priest offered me hot green tea before explaining why he had invited me halfway across the Big Island to meet him. The room was sparsely furnished with a wooden table and two wooden chairs. I felt the chair beneath me as I tried to become a Japanese of his generation, sipping tea by holding the tiny teacup with both hands and bowing to suggest humility and gratitude. Between us lay my book of poems, *Sand Grains*.

I had been living with both feet slightly off the ground since its publication, my first published book of poems. A six-year-old's dream, finally a reality. The *Honolulu Advertiser* devoted a page to its review. A bouquet of spring flowers from the mayor's office greeted me at the book signing. They called me, "poet." The blurb on the jacket cover read: *Here is a pervading sense of the essential aloneness of the human spirit, the core of being hidden behind a protective mask.* The poems were written as alternative to driving into a tree after the end of a first love relationship with Robert. Poem after poem examined the imperfection of men, the unfairness of life, my brokenness. I was young. I was searching for the woman I was to become. Why would any of that interest a Buddhist priest? Unless he wanted his book autographed?

Except for the sound of a nearby waterfall, the room was quiet. The old priest poured me a second cup of tea. I felt it settle in my stomach and spread through the rest of my body. He sat there carefully turning pages of my book, pausing now and then. I kept turning the teacup in my hands, waiting.

Finally, in halting English, he said, "Kakugawa-san, there is much pain in your life. Permit me to explain the difference between Western love and Eastern love. In Western love, when someone no longer loves you, you are taught to say, 'I must stop loving him since he doesn't love me back.' In Eastern love, we say, 'I will continue to love him whether he loves me or not.'" After a long pause, he added, "Listen to the sound of the water, Kakugawa-san. Listen, and learn to flow with it. Learn to love and live the Eastern way."

I walked away with undefinable joy. I wanted to weep for no reason at all. I wanted to embrace the entire world. Yes! I felt such freedom. Such power! I felt a huge burden of pain being lifted out of my body. I felt strong and wise. Yes, I'd follow the Eastern way. I'd follow the flow of the river. I would let go of that romantic notion of happily-ever-after found in novels and live life as it is. I would not be paralyzed any more.

I rushed home to write a letter to Robert. I wished him a happy life, thanked him for all the deep emotions I discovered I was capable of feeling. I felt magnanimously wise, perhaps even wiser than he.

I was young. My heart would be broken many more times. "When I am dead," I arrogantly said, "write this on my tombstone: She lived!"

Three more poetry books followed over the next three years. My pen anchored me, kept me attached to the worst and best of times. I was a poet, fearless, I thought, and a far cry from the person I was when I sipped tea with the Buddhist priest.

My poetry reflected this transformation, which came slowly and steadily. The process was not as easily done, as these poetry lines reveal:

>...my hungry heart beats,
>   alone...like little grey wrens
>   crying! to be fed...
>***
>...she blooms, then clings
>   till shriveled veins
>   slowly burn
>   her clutching hands...
>***
>...forgive the truth I offered you
> when I said I love you.
> I love you...
>***
>Do little fallen sparrows
>Damningly, painfully cry
>Of short-lived flights
>Over silver foiled lakes

And crayoned fields;
Or do little fallen sparrows
Happily, gratefully whisper
— I flew —
While dry dead leaves
Lightly touch their statued backs
As dusk slowly turns its head?

For twenty-eight years I floated buoyantly on the come-and-go river of love that the old priest had shown me. Whatever pain and grief accompanied love, there remained the poet, the essence of what I perceived my life to be. Then I hit a rock. Fear, anxiety and feelings of helplessness swirled around me like the eye of a hurricane. My mother had been diagnosed with Alzheimer's. I began to drown, loaded down with heavy gear, unable to swim this river that had become such a friend to me. I was barely treading water. How do I stop Alzheimer's? How do I stop this thief from invading my mother's life? How do I capture this thief who was leaving undecipherable chalk dust on my mother's brain? I found myself in a dry riverbed.

One otherwise ordinary day, ordinary meaning a norm for bottomless pits, I was stuck in traffic, driving my mother from her doctor's appointment, answering her repeated question, "Where are we going?"

"*Okaasan*," I groaned. "I don't know." She must have known it was time for silence because soon the only sounds were from the radio and impatient drivers hitting their horns. We sat in silence, waiting for traffic to move.

In our silence, the Buddhist priest appeared. Soon the sound of traffic was splashing on the rocks beneath a waterfall. The aroma of green tea filled the car. Flow with the river. Flow with the river. A horn honked; the light turned green. I took hold of the oar, drove off the next ramp and said, "*Okaasan*, let's go get some tea and dessert."

From then on, whenever an obstruction appeared, I embraced it. Whatever Alzheimer's stole, we lived without. Whatever time was taken, a few minutes were retrieved to sip tea and watch steam from the cup dissipate into the thin air. With my mother at my side, I listened to the sound of water and flowed to the end of our separate journeys with love, compassion and dignity, because in the East, water flows without obstruction.

Frances the Fraud: Part I

L et me introduce myself: I am Wordsworth, the Mouse Poet. If you attended a book signing for any of the five books Frances wrote about me, I may have had the pleasure of meeting you. Although I hesitate to admit it, I'm a good eavesdropper. One day I overheard her friend Red tell her, "You're such a fraud, your next book should be called *Frances the Fraud!*" Frances the Fraud! The idea intrigued me, so I decided to investigate and see what I could find or remember to support Red's claim. Well, did I unearth some dirt! She turned out to be one unforgettable, fraudulent character in my books. Frances may not appreciate me exposing her as a fraud; she may even try to sue me for slander. But I have to risk it: if she's a fraud, then all the stories she's written about me may be lies, and where would that leave me?

Did it begin with that Catholic priest who stopped her at age eight on her way to school and told her, "My poor child, you are going to hell. Only Catholics go to heaven." My investigation took many turns and curves. The priest didn't win her any Hail Mary's. Nor did that coax her into a fraudulent life; it was nothing that complicated. She just imagined things. The evidence for fraud that I uncovered comes down to three simple things: black stockings, red nail polish and her high school typing teacher.

The entire time Frances taught at elementary schools in Hilo, she was never asked to bring food to potluck dinners. "Bring the paper plates," the faculty would tell her. "That will be your contribution." Why would they assume she couldn't cook and let her get away so easily while others had to rush home after a long day's work to cook over a hot stove? I asked her colleague, and this is the story: She always wore black stockings to work and her nails were always painted red. Anyone who dresses like a clotheshorse surely must not spend time in the kitchen or maybe not even have a kitchen. How else could she keep those nails unchipped?

"Shhh," I heard her say to me, "I got a good deal going here. All I need is for you to be silent, Wordsworth." For years, she got away with paper plates and plastic forks, except for that one potluck where she was given a recipe. A colleague who would not be able to attend the potluck gave her a recipe for curried chicken and said, "Do you think you could follow this recipe and bring chicken to our potluck?"

"Sure," she slowly said, and took the recipe as though it was a sheet of used Kleenex. Another act deserving an Oscar.

I know Frances. She loves to explore her cooking skills with new recipes. Her kitchen wall has over fifty bottles of spices and herbs in addition to her herb garden.

"Shhhh, hush, never let it be known that I enjoy new recipes for family gatherings. Don't say a word about the Willows Restaurant recipe for orange duck I roasted for our family reunion. I'll tell you, that was a Martha Stewart moment." I'll tell you, her Julia Child recipe books are tattered with gravy spots and dog-eared pages. Paper plates? What a fraud, indeed!

A few years into teaching, she was asked by the State Department of Education to supervise the testing of the Hawaii English Program on the Big Island. Why Frances? It must be those black stockings again, looking oh soooo professional, and those red painted nails. On a less frivolous note, two educators, Elaine Kono and Margaret Oda, must be credited for seeing beyond her black stockings to open doors to positions Frances never thought possible at the state and district levels. She took the supervisory job which then led her to the Curriculum Center at the University of Hawaii, Oahu, where she had the privilege of joining other educators to create the State middle and high school literature program. She didn't have any graduate degree but she did have a few published books of poetry, so the fraud began again. Her application forms were altered to "master's degree or published books." They should have added black stockings with red painted nails or its equivalent.

I'm thinking of the story of her sister-in-law who confessed that when she was dating Frances's brother, her friends warned that she was dating someone whose sister wears stockings even on Saturdays. How would you like that for a sister-in-law? Not fraud exactly, but not a very good character reference either.

The stockings didn't always work in her favor. In Japan, there is a word, *bachi,* which means spiritual punishment from above. When she returned to the classroom after spending years at the state office, she was not well-received at an elementary school. She taught sixth graders and noticed a cool reception by other teachers. To the principal's request that she offer some writing and literature after-school workshops for the faculty, her answer was always no. "It's too early, I need to be accepted by the faculty." The principal kept asking, "When are you going to be ready?"

Finally one day, mid-year of her first year at the school, a teacher told her, "You do know that many teachers resent having you here?"

"Why?" Frances said, shocked.

"Everyone is assuming that because you came from the state office, your classroom has air conditioning. And that's privilege."

"Why would anyone think I have AC in my room, because I don't."

"You're the only one who wears stockings to work. Why would anyone wear stockings in this hot weather if she didn't have AC?" Frances assured her that her classroom was as hot as everyone else's and hoped she would put this on the coconut wireless.

Finally, after six years of not being truly accepted by the faculty, she agreed to become the writing resource teacher for the school and entered each classroom once a week. Those black stockings brought her astonishing encounters with one particular student.

"Oh no, oh no, teacher. Teacher, you are turning Black!" The cry greeted her one morning after she had entered a second-grade class. The child looked horrified and frightened.

"Keisha," Frances said, "Where am I turning Black?"

"Your legs, your legs," she said, pointing to Frances's legs.

"Oh Keisha," ran through Frances's head, "Is it that bad, being Black?"

She took Keisha's hand to her legs and explained, "Keisha, I'm wearing black stockings." Frances turned around and did a pirouette and said, "Keisha, I wear black stockings because they make me feel beautiful." Keisha, not convinced, walked away murmuring, "Why would anyone want to be Black?" Her black stockings gave Frances a window to help Keisha write poetry to explore that last comment.

Frances ended her career at the Honolulu District Office, visiting schools to help the faculties develop curricula within the Department of Education guidelines. She was still wearing her black stockings and red nail polish. One morning, the assistant superintendent and her supervisor, both males, called her in for a conference. "Now what have I done?"

The two men had the meeting well orchestrated and motioned her to sit on a chair facing both of them. "We are Barbara Walters and Charlie Rose," one began. "Pretend we are on TV. We noticed how well-dressed you are, so we are wondering, are you single, or do you have a boyfriend? We figured anyone who pays so much attention to her dress must be single."

Frances immediately resorted to her Kapoho outhouse survival skills: she stood, faced both men, said, "I'm sorry, but your time is up," and walked out.

How did a Kapoho country bumpkin become a clotheshorse? This edited excerpt from her book, *Teacher, You Look Like a Horse* may illustrate how a girl growing up in remote Kapoho with outhouses, water tanks, kerosene lamps and battery-run radios managed to become so fashion conscious.

> My decision to become a teacher was based on the only other alternative I thought was available at the time: becoming a prostitute. Perhaps I'd better explain.
>
> Kapoho, which lies buried under lava today on the Big Island of Hawaii, was my birthplace and childhood home. This little village had no electricity, no water system and no telephones except for the three party-line telephones located

in three of the four grocery stores. There was one generator-powered movie theater and tiny Kapoho School, a three-room facility with three teachers, none of whom had a college education. The eruptions would eventually bury everything we owned: kerosene lamps and stoves, kerosene-run refrigerators, gas irons, water tanks, out-houses, and our battery-run radio which brought to our village, such programs as *Arthur Godfrey, The Romance of Helen Trent, Young Dr. Malone* and *The Lone Ranger.*

Remote, yes, we were separated from the much larger town of Hilo by an hour's ride on an unpaved road, but we were not naïve innocents. "Prostitute" was a household word as familiar as "Christmas" and the "Easter Bunny."

We played barefoot on the dusty roads. We talked on our wire-connected tin-can phones. We gazed with wonder at the sight of sleek black cars carrying tall, high-heeled, heavily made-up women to the Filipino camps. Their high heels seemed almost stilt-like as they fought to keep their balance, walking up the gravel road to the camp. We may not have known exactly what prostitutes did, but from the whispers, we knew it was something dark and forbidden. After Pearl Harbor, we could see the USO girls, similarly dressed, entertaining soldiers camped in our village.

To me, their red nail polish and stylish clothes, hemmed above their knees symbolized elegance, sophistication, New York City: something, anything that was out-of-Kapoho.

One day, I secretly bought a bottle of red nail polish at Kress store in Hilo. I painted my pinky red, thinking one little painted pinky wouldn't be too evil or bad.

"Forget that," a maiden aunt told me. "Don't you know this is worse than ten painted nails? Don't you know prostitutes keep one nail longer than the others and painted red? It's a sure sign of their trade." Red polish was out from then on, forbidden fruit.

During my high school years at Pahoa High School, a typing teacher made me forget my aunt's words of warning. Every nail on both of her hands was painted red. I knew then and there that being a teacher, respected and important, gave one permission to wear red nail polish, in the fashion of prostitutes and other girls of questionable reputation. After that, it was my fervent dream to become the teacher with red nail polish.

Every morning, after getting off the bus, I stood on the second floor of the school to watch the parade of teachers walk from their teachers' cottages to the office. What a show of sophistication and dignity they presented: dresses, stockings and red nail polish. I knew then that I, too, would someday become one of them. And I did.

One of my favorite stories came from Sacramento where she posed as an attorney. Now if this isn't fraud, to pose as an attorney, I don't know what is.

This is her friend's story:

I was injured working in the postal department and needed my doctor's signature to get me workman's comp. My doctor kept delaying his signature because the U.S. Postal Department countered my report with doubts that I was injured at work. I was hurting both physically and financially when I told Frances my story. She said, "I'll go with you to your doctor as an attorney and I'm sure he'll sign the papers." She dressed in a suit, black stockings, carried her briefcase and we entered the doctor's office. Before I could introduce her, Frances took out her hand for a handshake and said, "I'm Frances, here for Marie." I had to keep from laughing. Throughout the visit, the doctor kept glancing at Frances as she vigorously wrote on her yellow pad. I got my papers signed, we walked out solemnly to my car and then burst into laughter and did a high five. Hey, she never said she was an attorney.

But the best is when I heard Frances say she wore black stockings for the sake of mankind. I say she was a great flirt. Look at one of her poems I found on her desk.

Black Stockings and a Pair of Red Heels

Anxious, I entered his room.
Bouquet of flowers instantly overpowered
By Lysol, Clorox, antiseptics.
A brilliant mind, A Harvard chemist,
Dulled by dementia.
Complicated by a fall.
A stranger many years ago,
A patron at the library.
His voice as the door closed behind me
Reciting an old poem of mine:
Under the rising sun
The enemy came
Wearing my face.
What poet
Wouldn't stop at such an entrance?
We'd meet for lunch now and then
Until the other woman,
Dementia, showed up.
For a split second that morning
Dressing for his visit
My once young, daring voice
Silenced the other.
He was propped up with pillows.
I offered him flowers.
He looked at me, ignored the flowers,
Smiled and said with a twinkle,
"Thank you for wearing black stockings."
I sat, crossed my legs, lifted my red heels,

Chatted my monologue
Until the other woman entered the room.

There are more stories to tell, and this alone will probably get my hands in handcuffs but I'm on a roll, so to speak, with Frances the Fraud Part II.

Frances the Fraud: Part II

This is Wordsworth again with another collection of stories on Frances the Fraud. She objects to being called a fraud and considers it "Kapoho Surviving Skills" or poetic license, so I'll let you judge this for yourself.

Frances was an avid reader, but can there be too much of a good thing? I think she may have learned more than the authors intended. Characters in some of her favorite books taught her how to use creativity and manipulation to manage situations to her best advantage. In her mind, I think she actually became those characters, characters who know exactly how to get out of situations, without red painted nails. Look at Hansel and Gretel, Charlotte's clever use of her web, and even Jack and the beanstalk.

Frances relied on books to avoid household chores. Whenever she heard, "Hideko! Come do the dishes!" or "Hideko! Time to cook the rice!" or "Hideko! Start the *furo*!" she escaped to the outhouse with a book or a copy of the *Reader's Digest*. Her voice, loud enough to be heard by passersby, announced, "I stay in the toilet, reading!" Or she sat on the porch with a book and shouted, "I reading a book!" Books meant education to her parents, and Frances knew they would not allow her siblings to interfere with her education. "Leave her alone, she's reading." Reading, or the appearance of reading, became her passport to avoid unwanted chores. She received support from villagers who saw her on the porch and commented, "You so lucky your children like to read."

Her sixth-grade teacher must have sensed she had a writer's imagination when, on the last day of school, she told her to "keep on writing." Earlier in the year, Frances had written a story about a young girl's yearning to be somewhere other than Kapoho.

> Once upon a time, there lived a girl whose classmates were very wealthy. Every September, on the first day of school, they talked about their summer travels to Paris, New York City and London. The girl listened in envy. The following summer while her friends traveled to all those faraway places, she spent her summer in the public library. When she returned to school in September, she told stories about her travels to Africa, India and Russia. She described each country, her favorite places and their people. She repeated a conversation between a Communist and herself in Moscow. No one ever discovered she had never left home.
>
> —from *Echoes of Kapoho*

In high school, she won first prize in a national shorthand contest sponsored by the Esterbrook Pen company. There is a photo of Frances receiving a fountain pen as a prize, with her proud shorthand teacher standing next to her. If only her teacher and the judges at Esterbrook Pen knew how she won this prize. She developed her own scribbles to replace some of the difficult shorthand to speed her translations because she struggled with the memorization. Her own scribbles weren't distinguishable from the real shorthand, so the teacher never caught her. She wrote dictations in her own simplified scribbles and transcribed them into English faster than anyone else. She would have made a fine stenographer.

Throughout her high school years, she often taught the Buddhist Sunday School when ministers were unable to make it to Kapoho. She didn't use any prescribed Buddhist texts for her lessons. In her eyes, they were boring, stale stories of Buddha's young life, told and retold in awkward translations by every minister whose English was their second language. As ministers delivered these barely understandable sermons, students wandered off into their own fantasy worlds and learned nothing. Instead of using the standard texts, Frances chose stories from *Our Romance, Good Housekeeping* and *Reader's Digest*. She ended each story with a Buddhist lesson, fashioning acts of kindness and compassion. "This is what it means to be a Buddhist," was the moral of each story. On Monday mornings, after the bus dropped the Kapoho students off at Pahoa School, and before classes began, Frances repeated and embellished those same stories for classmates who eagerly waited for their weekly *True Confessions* tales in a hallway corner.

We all know how she received an A in her college music class without knowing a single musical note and by turning in a blank final exam. This is lifted from her *Echoes of Kapoho* book:

There Was a Man Named Levi

I sat in terror in Professor Levi's Basic Music Course at the University of Hawaii. I was the only one with panic on her face. I looked at the others sitting around me, and they were nodded in understanding agreement with everything the professor said. My Kapoho had failed me once again, even before the first class hour was over.

My mother didn't like this story I retold often as an adult. Why would I repeat a story she found unpleasant? Was I insinuating my Kapoho parents had failed me by not getting me a violin? One day by pure accident I heard violin music pour out of our battery-run radio. I felt so moved, I knew I wanted to create something similar and equally beautiful. I found a broomstick and sawed it down to violin length. We rarely heard violin music on our radio, but when we did, it transformed my world. I held the broomstick under my chin and pretended I was the violinist, playing for hours in the living room. Now that was pretty easy, the shortened broomstick tucked under my chin and an imaginary bow moving across the invisible strings as my body swayed along in rhythm. Soon I didn't need the radio; I played the broomstick with the music pouring out of my head.

My sister had something better going for her. She took piano lessons in Hilo, came home and practiced on imaginary keys when she came home. Her fingers flew over invisible keys, pausing when she made an error or stumbled over some notes. She was always ready for her next lesson in Hilo. She was later allowed to use the piano in the Community Hall for an hour a day.

I continued to play my broomstick.

Professor Levi's voice was barely audible above my pounding heart.

"The finals," he said, "will be pretty standard." He waved a blank music sheet at us and continued, "I'll play a few chords on the piano and you will simply add in the notes."

It was back to the cane fields for me. How was I going to pass the required music course to get my teaching diploma? Ellen and Ella, both Hilo High graduates with years of piano lessons behind them, sat calmly as they awaited the final. But I still knew nothing about musical notation.

How were my years of listening to Arthur Godfrey and his ukulele going to help me now? I did sing in the high school chorus, but that was the extent of my musical education beyond my broomstick fantasies. You can see why I needed to get out of Kapoho and into a world with more opportunities. Madame Pele, you came too late. If you had inundated Kapoho a few years earlier, who knows how my musical future might have developed?

Yet here I was, basically ignorant but needing to pass this course. *What am I going to do?* I never knew fear could manifest as physical pain in my gut or as gasping breath. I wanted to forget my dreams and go home.

The professor was the epitome of an old maestro: His white hair curled around the nape of his neck, his handlebar moustache was well-oiled and precisely pointed. The image he presented to his young, naïve students was both intimidating and awe-inspiring.

I attended class for a few weeks, feeling like an alien. I took no notes and merely listened, hating every moment and knowing I was failing. Then one night, alone in my room, where I was working as a live-in maid, my Kapoho survival skills kicked in. I began to develop Plan A with the desperation of a fish out of water. Writing being one of my loves, I went to class early and left a hand-written poem on Professor's Levi's desk. I watched his face as he read the poem, saw a glint of pleasure there and knew my course of action. He was ready for Plan B.

About a week later, I stood up in class before he could begin and announced, "Professor, I wrote you a poem and I'd like to read it." I had been carrying that verse for weeks in my handbag. It was now or never.

Sometimes, the planets will be aligned perfectly and the gods begin their day with kindness in their hearts for the desperate and the scared. I read my poem and the class applauded. Mr. Levi asked for the copy of the poem. From the look on his face, I knew it wasn't through his piano that I was going to pass.

I wrote him poems throughout the semester. Now and then I would read them in class, but most of them were left on his desk. Once I daringly left a poem with a stem of red rose, much to his delight.

The finals were just as he had explained on the first day of class. He passed out blank music sheets to the class, went to the piano and played a few chords. I watched Ella and Ellen fill their lines with notes, as did the rest of the class. I sat and trembled, too distraught to even think of copying my neighbor's notes. The Russian poets, I read somewhere, were feared more than the KGB. "Oh, please let my pen be as powerful," I prayed. I handed in a blank sheet, folded over twice.

On the last day of class, he followed me out and said, "I need to speak to you."

"Oh shit, please God, let me pass."

He took both my hands in his and said, "You make me feel I was born too soon."

I giggled, for I was only eighteen years old, and walked away. I had an A for the course and was on my way to a college degree. Or so I thought, until I took Speech 100 and that fear of failure threatened me again.

Fifty-six years later, I was autographing books at a bookshop in Honolulu. I sensed someone standing in front of me, and before I could look up, I heard a voice reciting:

> There was a man named Levi
> Whose hair was white and wavy.
> But when his fingers hit the ivories
> There was music smoother than gravy.

"I was in Professor Levi's class with you," she explained. "I never forgot you and the poems you read in class. I always admired you and thought you were someone so special, so independent and confident."

In her senior year of college, Frances pulled a fast one in her children's literature class. As part of the finals, each student had to read a children's book to the class. Students were to play-act as children and respond accordingly. The professor often interrupted the reading with off-the-wall comments to see how the students would handle them. *"Teacher, he's bothering me. Teacher, are there pictures? Teacher, I need to use the bathroom."* When it was Frances's turn, knowing how difficult some of the questions would be, she started with: *"You are all mute children."* The professor shook her head with a knowing smile on her face. Frances read the story without any interruptions. After the story, she took full control by asking, *"Did you like the story?"* Nods. *"Did you think the character was wise in what she did?"* Nods. She got another A.

Her elementary school teachers had often shaken their heads, too. "Use this week's spelling words in a sentence," was a regular assignment. Frances didn't know what "meticulous" meant, not having done her homework with the dictionary, so she wrote: *The teacher asked me to use meticulous in a sentence.* She got away with it—more than once. She did use it in a sentence, didn't she?

Maybe writers know how to create mountains out of molehills or know how to develop and expand a small incident into an epic? Frances is known as a hula dancer, outside of Hawaii. Yet she knows how to dance one song; yes, only one song called "Yellow Ginger Lei."

When she taught in Michigan for a year, she danced "Yellow Ginger Lei" at a PTA meeting and became known as the Hawaiian dancer. She was invited to perform at a national Girl Scout Conference where she danced, once again, "Yellow Ginger Lei" around the gymnasium filled with Girl Scouts from Canada and the U.S. For most of the girls, this was their first hula performance.

In Sacramento, when she heard of a resident at a nursing home who still spoke of her visits to Hawaii, what did Frances do but go to a Dollar Store, purchase plastic lei and a couple of grass skirts to fit around her waist and entertained the delighted residents to the one and only dance she knew: "Yellow Ginger Lei."

One weekend at Hotel Molokai on the island of Molokai, the Molokai Trio asked her to join them in a dance. They became the Molokai Foursome, and Frances danced around the pool and in a dining room, entertaining tourists who didn't know any better. When asked for an encore, she sheepishly told the Trio the truth.

I think I've dug enough dirt, so to speak. I'll turn the pen over to Frances and let her finish her stories. This was fun, writing behind her back. Psst, if you know of any stories, send them to me.

Wordsworth: It's My Turn Now

Wordsworth has said a lot of things about me. Even if my pursuit of my goals took a few minor deceptions to achieve from time to time, his stories here remind me of things I did that I didn't even think I could do. So maybe this is a good time to tell you a story about Wordsworth and a great accomplishment of his that he didn't know he could do.

I was a long way from Kapoho. Look at all that traffic outside. No cane fields and unpaved roads here. I can't believe I am sitting in the College Inn near UH waiting for the publisher who is interested in my Wordsworth the Poet *book. This is like being in a movie about me. "Oh wow," I said to myself, as a man came walking towards my table. "That must be the publisher."*

The man stopped and introduced himself. It was him. Before I could get a word out, he said, "You are very beautiful." I murmured, "Thank you." Then he took one of my old books of poetry out of his briefcase and laid it down on the table. "I read some of your poems and find them very Japanese and elegant. One of my favorites is "Sunday Afternoon." Will you read it to me?" He handed me a copy of *Golden Spike*.

I better play this right. Japanese and elegant. I can do this. I better not mess this up.

I took the book and read:

Sunday Afternoon

Silence grows louder,
Raindrops fall longer.
Clouds drop lower,
Winds sing gentler.
Rooms feel emptier,
The heart aches deeper.
The grass stands colder,
Steps walk slower.
It's Sunday
In the afternoon.

"That poem always gets to me," the publisher said. "You captured Sunday afternoons just perfectly."

I can't believe this. He even likes my poems! Wordsworth the Poet, I whispered in my mind, we are on a roll. We are going to be published! Maybe you'll even get the Caldecott Prize. Wouldn't that be something? We gotta think big, Wordsworth.

The publisher continued, "I've got one of the best illustrators working for me. He's done all my children's books and he's delighted with your story, too."

Hear that, Wordsworth? They like you. Yipppeee.

"Are you ready to order?" he gently asked.

"Yes," I said. "Thank you."

I pretended not to hear him say under his breath, "She is so Japanese and subtle."

Pinch me, Wordsworth. Am I in a movie scene with a happy ending? This is big time.

I had four poetry books published by a company in Texas. It was all arranged through the mail. I never met the publisher or editor in person. Now I was sitting with a real live publisher who was interested in my work. That was certainly a step out of the outhouse in Kapoho.

We discussed the book and some of the details of having it published. Then he called out for the waitress who was just finishing writing the tab for another table

"Hey! You!" he called, "Come here. We're ready to order." He looked at me and said, "Sheez, hope she understands English!"

The waitress came to our table with a forced smile, the kind I sometimes have when I feel I'm being treated rudely but don't want to pick a fight openly.

The publisher didn't even bother to look at her when he abruptly said, "Get us some coffee first, then we will order lunch." His brusqueness caught me by surprise. Was this the same man who had just showered me with praise and respect? Someone who liked my poems and therefore liked me, but he was treating another person who had done him no harm with such rudeness?

I was torn. I wanted so much to admire this person who

thought my book was worthy of publishing. That was when I heard Wordsworth.

"Oh, Frances," Wordsworth whispered, "Can you really want to put me in the hands of someone with such little respect for others? After all, the only difference between you and that poor waitress are your jobs. Why, if he saw you in the cane fields of Kapoho, he wouldn't even stop to give you the time of day. How can you let him publish our book?"

"But Wordsworth, this is our big chance to be published. Remember how you got here. I wrote you five years ago to enter you in a contest sponsored by the Hawaii State Foundation on Culture and the Arts. You came in second place. Second place, Wordsworth. I spent that $100 check many times over. Wordsworth, this is our big chance."

"How can you let a man who stands for everything we are not publish this book? Remember how YOU got here. Think back, Frances, think back when the only difference between you and the enemy was your face."

"I haven't forgotten, Wordsworth. That day changed my face forever with that, 'Hey Jap.' I know all that. Right now, we got to focus on why we're here."

"Well, welcome to the Pearl Harbor Café, Frances."

"I don't need a comedian right now."

"Remember, too, Frances, that Catholic priest who told you you were going to Hell for not being Catholic. Remember how you felt? Or even those years when you were working as a live-

in maid to support yourself in college."

"Gee, Wordsworth. Why bring that up. I took care of that priest in college. Sure, I felt like a second-class citizen, eating in the kitchen and having cold slices of roast beef the day after their dinner parties. But this is publishing, Wordsworth."

"And there was the Uyeda Store. Remember? Tell me the story again."

The waitress walked away with our order. He looked through the manuscript, nodding.

"All right. All right. I'm walking past Uyeda Store on my way home from school when I hear my name. There are four issei men and women sitting in front of the store. I heard them say, 'The Kakugawa children are all smart, they'll be very successful. But the middle one, Hideko, that one won't amount to much. Yes, that one is different.'

'You just wait,' I told them in my head, 'someday all of you will be waiting in line to buy my books because I'm going to be a writer!' And they did."

"All right, Frances. How about D-U-M-B?"

"You don't quit, do you? So, my fifth and sixth grade teacher's favorite words were, 'Some people's children are so d-u-m-b.' Each time I gave an incorrect answer or offered an off-the-wall opinion, I was crowned d-u-m-b. I didn't care, Wordsworth, because I knew she, too, would someday be waiting in line to buy my books, most likely behind the people from Uyeda Store, and she was."

"Frances," I heard the publisher say. "Do you want dessert? More coffee?"

"No, no, thank you."

"Everything looks good. I'll be dropping off the contract in a couple of days. We've got a winner here. We'll get started on the illustrations as soon as you sign the contract."

"That waitress felt just like you in all your stories, Frances," Wordsworth continued.

"That waitress has to learn to get a thick skin, Wordsworth. I did. I worked hard to get out of Kapoho and this book will take me further away."

"Maybe you're too far away, Frances."

The publisher left a dollar tip on the table and walked me out, his hand gently leading me out the door. We shook hands on the sidewalk and as I walked toward my car, I heard Wordsworth.

"Frances!" Wordsworth said loudly in my head, "Frances, how can you even consider giving me over to this guy? Maybe you forgot your friend Richard Lyman, who helped you and everyone else in Kapoho and didn't care one bit where they came from, whose ancestry they had or what they did for a living, as long as they were honest people with integrity and compassion for others. Are you forgetting what Mr. Lyman was really telling you when he gave you that first scholarship and put you on the road to success?"

Wordsworth was right, of course. But still the thought of letting this one opportunity slip through my fingers pulled on me. Do I return Wordsworth to my desk drawer again? But this is my big chance. That waitress must learn there will always be rude people around who will treat you like a non-person. She has nothing to do with my chance of having my first children's book published. I should add, maybe a prize-winning children's book.

Was it really so important who or what this guy was, as long as my first book of stories got published? After all, I didn't really know the people in Texas who published my poetry. Yes, they said some nice things about my work, but did I really know if any of them would treat a waitress any differently that this guy did? Did it matter?

I put duct tape on Wordsworth's mouth and drove home.

We stayed up most of the night on a see-saw, Wordsworth and I.

I could hear Wordsworth. *"Frances, if you let this man publish* Wordsworth the Poet *I will be ashamed to even have my name on the book, and so will you. It's not who we are, and it won't take us where we want to be. I can wait and so can you for the right time and the right people."*

Late next morning I called the publisher and asked for my manuscript back. "You're making a big mistake," he said. "Call me if you change your mind," and he was abruptly gone, speaking to the waitress once again. I was no longer the beautiful poet. I returned Wordsworth back to my desk and there he waited for thirty years. Yes, it took thirty more years before the right time and the right people finally did come along.

I sat across from George Engebretson of Watermark Publishing, going over the final phase of publishing my *Teacher, You Look Like a Horse* book. I took a deep breath and with fingers crossed and shaking, I took out *Wordsworth the Poet*.

"Okay, Wordsworth, this is our chance."

"George, I want to read you a little story."

Without giving George a second to reply, I began to read. I looked at his face between paragraphs; his face was of that of poker player who had a bad hand.

"He doesn't like it. Oh shoots, Wordsworth, at least I tried."

I put the story down, and was unprepared to hear him say, "This is delightful, Frances. I want to do this story. I see a whole series of Wordsworth books."

Wordsworth and I danced our way home with Wordsworth saying, *"He is everything the other publisher was not. Yes, yes, yes."* We kept our vow to make Wordsworth a work of spotless integrity, compassion and dignity, from the first mark I made on the page, to the last copy off the press.

Wordsworth the Poet was followed by four other books in the series and each received a Best Children's Story award in the year of their publication. The first two Wordsworth stories were presented in a live stage musical by the University of Hawaii, Hilo, Performing Arts Center in 2022. It took almost twenty years since its publication to have Wordsworth sing his poetry on stage.

More importantly than his awards, Wordsworth has made a difference for children. Through his books, young readers have made changes in their families, respecting and embracing their elders, asking for artificial Christmas trees instead of cutting down another tree, conversing with friends and family members without their electronic devices, and becoming poets.

And now I'll tell you a little secret about Wordsworth. That awful night of indecision about whether to go with the first publisher, Wordsworth said he didn't know if he could do it. He said he knew how much I wanted to publish him, and he didn't think he had it in him to get in my way and stop me from taking the road he knew was the wrong one to take. But he did it anyway, even though he didn't know he could. I'd say that pretty much makes Wordsworth a good friend to have around.

The Gentleman from Kapoho

I sat next to Richard Lyman, Jr., on Easter Sunday, 1981, at the Oahu Country Club with his wife, Jane, and daughter and son-in-law, the Francis Kealas. I had interviewed Mr. Lyman at his home earlier that day. I wanted to know who this man was, he who had given me the first ticket out of Kapoho.

I was a senior in high school in 1954 from the village of Kapoho on the Big Island of Hawaii; Kapoho, where nights were lighted by kerosene lamps, refrigerators ran by kerosene wicks, and outhouses stood alongside every home, for there was no water system or electricity.

"No college," my father had repeated often. "Educating girls is a waste of money since girls all get married in the end." That was his way of saying, "We can't afford to send you to college." My father earned about $200.00 a month. Just barely enough to support a family of seven with the oldest in college. I had dreams stronger than the realities of life. I secretly planned to defy my father.

One morning I did not get off the bus at Pahoa High School but rode into Hilo to the University of Hawaii. I got a live-in maid's job with a family of five. I had already been accepted at the University. I was all set, with or without my father's approval. On high school graduation night, I was surprised to receive the In Memory of Mother Lyman Scholarship, the first scholarship given by Richard Lyman, Jr.

My father no longer spoke of the uselessness of educating girls, for if Richard Lyman, the most respected name in Kapoho, would approve of college for me, then there must be something right in this. The University of Hawaii Alumni scholarship was also presented to me.

My first tuition was paid with this check from the Lyman scholarship. Years later, I realized how he had also given dignity rather than charity through that scholarship. Every summer, until I graduated, he would drop by, walking up the two wooden steps of our porch. Our conversations repeated themselves like a tape for four summers:

Lyman (holding my hand in both of his, a soft hidden twinkle in his eyes): "You got any boyfriends?"

Me: "No."

Lyman: "Good. No boyfriend. You finish school first."

In 1975, Richard Lyman received his own award, The Second Order of the Sacred Treasure from the Japanese government. I read about it in the newspapers and sent him a congratulatory note. That was my first contact with him since the summers of the fifties. He responded with a letter saying, "When I said 'No boyfriend,' I didn't mean for you to take this advice forever. Nothing would please me more than to receive a wedding invitation from Frances Kakugawa." He also congratulated me for the four books of poetry I had published and asked for copies.

His name always brought tears of joyous remembrance to my mother. She had sewn all the Lyman men's pants along with other villagers. My father, a Democrat, had campaigned for him, a Republican, during those years when he had run for public office, and had always kept one vote for him.

Who is this man, Richard Lyman? How did he get to Kapoho? Why is he so special to the villagers of Kapoho? What is it about him that puts him above the stereotypes of white plantation owners and which had won the trust and respect of the people of Kapoho? Why, after all these years, was he called back by the villagers, who now live in Pahoa, to share the highlights of their lives? When he was hospitalized, I received a call from my mother, concerned about his recovery. Our eighty-five-year-old neighbor flew to Oahu to visit him in the hospital. Who IS this man? I asked to have my questions answered by the man himself.

He was eight years old when his family moved to Kapoho in 1911 because his grandfather had died, and his uncles, who owned one thousand acres of cane and ranch land in Kapoho, had asked his father, Richard Lyman, Sr., to manage the lands of the estate. This father was called Bulldog Lyman behind his back by the villagers. He sat on his porch collecting rent from the villagers. My mother repeated often how she once had to pay rent twice in a month because she had lost her receipt and Lyman Sr. would not accept her story.

"I started school at Kapoho. When I got to the sixth grade, I had to go to Hilo. In those days, we had railroads running from Kapoho to Hilo. After I got through with grammar school, I almost didn't make it into high school because I couldn't speak proper English. I didn't know the difference between a noun and a pronoun. I didn't know the difference between a verb and an adverb. They tell me that they don't teach that anymore, but because of that, there was a question of whether I could go on to high school. But they said that I could try, so I went to Hilo High School. That was 1917, and I graduated in 1921.

"Then came time to think about what I was going to do—should I go to school, or should I go to work? In those days, ninety dollars a month was a tremendous amount of money, and I was given an opportunity to work for the plantation. For ninety dollars a month I almost took it, but my family decided that at least one member should go to college, and so I came to Oahu to attend the University of Hawaii. I graduated in 1925. It was then time to go to work.

"I had a chance to earn ninety dollars a month working at Hilo Boarding School as a house father. It didn't sound exciting to me, so Dad said, 'Well, go find yourself a job if you don't like that kind of job.'

"During that period, they were building the Hilo breakwater. Most of the rocks for that breakwater came from Kapoho. So I went over to see Mr. Roger James, who was the boss man. He said, 'Yes, boy, I'll give you a job. How much? Well, I'll give you twenty cents an hour.'

"So I reported to work. He said, 'Go and get some lime and spread it around the outhouses.' So I did it. 'Now, go heat up some hot water, mix it with creolin and go spread it on the walls and get rid of the bed bugs.' I did it. 'Now grab a shovel.' Now all those years I went to school, nobody had shown me how to use a shovel. So he came down into the quarry pit and said, 'You want to work here?' Well, when he showed me that there was a way to use the shovel, he became, in my estimation, the smartest man in the world.

"Another time he said, 'Now grab a sledgehammer and help those guys bust up those rocks and put them on the skip.' So I grabbed the sledge hammer, went down, started hitting the rocks with the hammer and nothing happened. So he came down again and again and said, 'Eh, boy, you want to work here?' And again I said, 'Yes, sir!' He said, 'Well, let me show you.' So he put on his eyeglasses and tapped the rock; the rock split. I thought, 'This man is smart.' And I realized he must have been smart because I got twenty cents an hour or eight dollars a week, thirty dollars a month, but *he* got five hundred dollars a month. And he had a house and a houseboy who also made him some *okolehao* for home use.

"Yet this man James couldn't read, and he couldn't write. He'd say, 'Hey, son, I forgot my glasses. I have a letter here.' I would read the letter for him. 'Thank you.' I thought, 'Well, poor guy, he didn't have his glasses so he couldn't read.' And another time, 'My hands are all dirty. I have a check here. Now if you sign my name, I'll put a little *x* here and I won't dirty my check.' Well, his hands *were* dirty. That was how smart he was. All I knew was that this man knew his job so well, I didn't even think about why I had to read his letters or why I had to sign his name on his checks."

Richard Lyman was promised by Mr. James that he would become a big shot, but he quit his job the day three Koreans were killed in an explosion of blasting powder as they were dynamiting the rocks. "They were so badly burned that their skin, fingernails, everything came off like a glove. I did not want to be a big shot. At that time I was a fireman on a donkey engine."

So Richard Lyman became a school teacher. He taught on Kauai, then on Oahu before returning to Hilo. From Hilo, he returned to Kapoho. There, in 1940, Mrs. Giacametti, a principal, told him to return to Honolulu to take a test to become a principal. "I don't want to be a principal; I don't want to be an old maid," was his answer. But he returned to Ewa School on Oahu until December 6, 1941.

"I had two uncles in the Army. That night, December 6, we had dinner at Ewa, and we had decided that I would visit them at Schofield barracks on December 7 to watch a football game. I recall December. There was a picture of the guards on alert in the newspaper, for they had alerted the troops. All that night was unusual to me: the radio was on a Hawaiian theme, and that, to me, was strange. Then came December 7. I knew I couldn't go back to teaching. All the men were going to war, and I wasn't going to be the only male left behind."

Richard Lyman tried to join the USED, a group of civilians trained to go to the South Pacific islands to do work that the regular troops would not do. But he was rejected because "I had a broken finger, and with a broken finger, the doctors said I could not pull a trigger. The doctors were so mixed up, they didn't know the difference between a broken finger on the wrong hand and the ability to shoot with the other."

So he tried to join the 442nd Infantry Regiment and the 100th Battalion. But he was rejected because he couldn't speak Japanese and he was "too old," thirty-four years old.

He then went to the CBs (Construction Battalion), a group organized by the navy to send men to the South Pacific to do what the USED was going to do. He spoke to the admiral.

"What can you do?"

"Well, I can plant things and make them grow."

"Do you think you can make grass grow on somebody's coral island?"

"Oh, sure, that won't be too hard. Mo' bettah you let me do it the way I think it can be done. Instead of throwing all your waste away, if you'll incorporate it with your coral sand, I'm sure we can get grass to grow."

"Well, that's fine. Sign this application."

But he was rejected by the admiral's supervisor, who was a commander in the navy. He was told they didn't need any broken-down farmers; they needed carpenters and electricians. So in 1942, Richard Lyman returned to agricultural work.

He went to Molokai to help raise corn, but the two thousand acres of corn produced a deficit because the Office of Price Control had set a limit on the price of corn and left no allotment for profit. Still, wanting to get into the war effort, in 1944, he got transferred to the Department of Interior and was sent to Guam to work on what was called "Economic Development." He stayed there until the end of the war, returning home in 1946.

"During that period, I found out that the Americans were the most stupid people when it came to dealing with aboriginal people. They expected the people to be able to speak English just like they were able to and expected them to read and write just like they could read and write, and I saw what had happened to Hawaii a long time ago was happening all over again. Like, within days after landing on Yap, they had the women covered, and the men in pants and shirts, and even shoes. You know, it was almost funny. The women of Yap thought brassieres were to be used like sunshades or blinders that are put on horses."

"Why do they have to wear those shoes?"

"Their feet are cracked."

"That's not unusual. Anybody who goes barefooted is going to have cracked feet."

"I had cracked feet when I was growing up. The Americans are always itching, scratching, perspiring with *kaki'o* (impetigo) over their bodies while the natives...no shirt, skin dry, why?"

So Richard returned to Kapoho after the 1946 tidal wave. At that time, one of his uncles had died, and the family's acres of Kapoho land were up for sale. Richard Lyman returned to settle his uncle's estate.

He had a dream that maybe he could buy the land and sell to each person that he or his parents had developed. But he had no money. Then one day a Japanese villager called Nakamura came to talk to him.

"Mr. Lyman, why don't you buy this land?"

"Because I don't have any money."

"Well, get two other men, they don't have money and they want to buy."

"How do you know?"

"They came to ask me if I would buy my store, if I would buy my house, and if I would buy my cane field."

"Well, look. If that man had an office on one side of the road and I had one on the other side of the road, where would you go?"

"I would see you."

"Why me?"

"I know you. I don't know that other man."

"Okay, you think people would be willing to buy?"

"Yes."

So Richard Lyman borrowed money, purchased his family's now more than a thousand acres of land and sold it back to the people of Kapoho. He sold not only land that they had built their homes on, but also land that they had gone out to work on, either for themselves or with their parents. (My parents bought thirteen acres of cane land and a half-acre house lot for about $350 an acre.) Many years later, Richard Lyman was approached by the son of a man who had bought land at this time.

"Mr. Lyman, I hope you don't get angry."

"Why?"

"My father had bought some land from you. My mother sold it."

"Would you mind telling me how much she got for it?"

"She got $1,800 an acre."

"Well, I'm happy. If you told me that she got paid about $250 an acre, then I would be unhappy."

"There were some cane fields at $100 an acre which nobody wanted because that land produced only about twenty tons of sugar cane, so I said to my brother, 'Well, we'd better get out and do it ourselves.'"

So Richard Lyman and his brothers bulldozed, cleared and planted. That crop brought in *eighty* tons of sugar cane an acre.

After a volcanic eruption in Kona, again, Richard Lyman began to think—what do you have to do to make things grow on lava rock? So, at the Constitutional Convention in 1949, where he was a delegate, a resolution was introduced, asking the University of Hawaii to do some research on this question. His first encounter with the dean from the College of Agriculture killed the resolution.

"What do you want us at the University to do?"

"We want you to do some research."

"But how are we going to do research? You did not appropriate any money."

"You mean to tell me you need money? What do you need money for?

"We need to analyze the rocks."

"You mean to tell me, after all these years, you don't know what's in a rock? Okay, let's go back to the old timers and see what they did." They planted papaya on land that was supposedly "junk," and today, most of the papaya growing out of rocks are found in the Puna area, on land considered "junk" land.

Richard Lyman has always shown respect for the little man all his life—the little man to whom he has gone for knowledge and advice, the little man whose voice he has listened to.

"In 1942, I was a county extension service agent for the University of Hawaii on Molokai. Extension agents go around telling people what to do, and how they should do things. So I would say to farmers, 'Maybe you should save some of your cauliflower seed,' or 'Maybe you should raise more papaya on Molokai.' I guess this one farmer got sick and tired of being told what to do, so he said to me, 'Suppose so good, why you no make?' Well, when he put it that way, I thought to myself, 'Yes, he's telling me something. Don't go telling people what to do. Go do it. And if it works, they will do it, too.'"

This philosophy seems to have started the papaya and sugar cane industry in lava-rock country in Puna. "So many things happen this way, you know. No sense talking. If you believe in something, do it. Show how it is done and not talk too much."

Richard Lyman ran for public office during the 1950s. He was a member of the last Territorial Senate and a member of the first State Senate. It was a simple question from a Japanese farmer who challenged him to run for office. "How come you don't run for Supervisor? You scared you going lose?"

This is my story of Richard Lyman, Jr., who helped to make many dreams come true. As for many families who had lived in Kapoho, there would be Lyman stories to be told, for each family would have their own. Like Mr. Henry Uyeki, a ninety-year-old neighbor, who was the first to receive US citizenship in Kapoho. On that memorable day, he chose the name Henry to be his new American name—after Richard Lyman's uncle Henry Lyman.

We grew up with our own Lyman stories. My mother sewed all the pants for the Lyman men, so I often saw them being measured by the square ruler in our living room. While we were young, my mother would find an Easter basket at our doorstep on Easter morning. Until my interview with Richard Lyman on this Easter Sunday, it was only speculation that the Easter Bunny was Richard Lyman.

"Your asking me this is like asking, 'Do you wash your face in the morning?'" What was so natural and ordinary to Richard Lyman was so precious to my mother that it had become a treasured memory.

During my interview, I had one over the Lyman family when he confessed, "I always drank water from the tap with my teeth clenched together to sieve the mosquito wigglers out."

"We," I bragged, "we had Bull Durham bags attached to the faucet to catch those wigglers!" What a revelation that the Kakugawa water was purer than the Lyman water.

The first-generation Japanese men took in Richard Lyman as their son. Once, they decided he needed a wife, so they arranged to have a bride sent from Japan. That didn't work out, and the marriage was annulled and the bride was returned to Japan. They later, as legend has it, introduced him to his present wife, Jane.

"That's all," he said. "That's the way it was."

But that was not all for Richard Lyman as he looked toward geothermal energy in the Puna area on lands that were considered unusable at one time.

"Well, that'll be the next chapter."

Richard Lyman's roots are there in the people of Kapoho. They seem to have started many years ago when Richard Lyman lost his father.

"After the funeral, I found envelopes with cash from all the villagers. I was very embarrassed. I didn't know what to do, so I asked a Japanese man, 'What should I do? These people need this money more than I do.'

He answered, 'You take the money but remember where it came from.'"

In 1969, when my father died, we received letters from Richard Lyman and his brother, each with *koden* (a monetary gift given at funerals) enclosed.

Richard Lyman remembered. I, too, have not forgotten, and paid him forward by giving a scholarship to a graduating senior at Pahoa School in the name of my mother, Matsue Kakugawa.

After my mother's death in 2002, I sold the cane field that had been left unattended since the 1960 eruption. A few acres were under lava rock. The Realtor was stunned. "I didn't know there are people like this anymore. Honestly, I didn't think I could sell your property because there is no public access road to the property except for one privately owned road. When they heard the name "Kakugawa," they allowed, in writing, free access to the property."

"Who owns that road?" I asked.

"The Lyman Estate," said the Realtor.

To My Father

Otosan, this is my first poem about you.
To an umbilical cord
That never existed between us.
I have pages of poems
Of *Okasan* but none for you.
I was 27, leaving for Michigan
To a new teaching position.
"If anyone is mean to you, come straight home."
The Miss Know-It-All daughter
Wanted to say, "I'm not a child.
I can take care of myself."
I managed to keep silent.
Three months later, on a plane,
Clutching a letter, heading home.
You had cancer and were dying.
That was the meanest thing I had ever heard.
Silence would have been better.

In novels, fathers and daughters often show affection for each other. They have conversations and hugs that are remembered for a lifetime. Fond recollections appear in memoirs and stories repeated generation after generation. All I have are sporadic conversations that didn't even come with hugs.

I was on my way to the Hilo airport for a flight to Jackson, Michigan, where I would live with my pen pal Kay Goff and her family while teaching first grade at Flora List Elementary School. Kay and I were pen pals during high school and we were meeting for the first time. Her husband, a banker, had worked with the Board of Education to get me that job.

Before I left, you said, "Since you speak English, I know you won't have trouble." Followed by, "If anyone is mean to you, come straight home." Instead of reassuring you that yes, I would do exactly that, I pointed to the door and said, "See this door? I'm going to bring home a tall, handsome, haole husband, so make it higher."

You chuckled and said, "Say anything you want."

Three months later, I received a letter saying you had "open and shut" surgery for cancer and there was nothing to be done. I stood in the Goff living room and showed the letter to Kay, who knew from my face that something was wrong. She read the letter and tried to hug me but I pushed her away, got into my car and drove through the countryside among trees holding brilliant red and orange and gold leaves. How could the world be so vibrant with colors when you were dying?

I wrote letters home saying, "Don't tell him he has cancer. He will not be able to handle it." Why I saw you as a weak man who would be devastated by such news, I don't know. You would prove me wrong.

In December, I received another letter saying you had weeks to live. The Board of Education met to give me leave with pay, the principal arranged for a substitute teacher and on the last day, parents came in with cookies and treats for a going home party. Over the intercom, I heard the song, "I'll Be Home for Christmas."

From Detroit to Hilo airport, casual conversations from seat companions assumed I was going to Hawaii for a vacation, lucky me. "My father is dying," froze in my mouth like icicles hanging from eaves.

During the long drive from Hilo airport to home, my sister, Momoe, warned me to not expect the same father. He is thin and bed-ridden, on pureed food, she warned. I stood outside your bedroom, afraid to enter. From the doorway, I heard you say, "I didn't have time to fix the door."

"Oh no," I said, "He's going to hit his head." And with laughter I entered the room.

"There's *manini* in the freezer for you," you added. You had asked your friend Togo-san to fish for manini, my favorite fish. I couldn't eat the fish, knowing you were on pureed food. I wanted to eat your pureed food instead and had problems chewing and swallowing the manini.

The second day you said, "I'll bet there are good doctors on the mainland."

"If there are," I said, "I would take you anywhere on the

mainland, but they have no cure for what you have." You nodded, satisfied that even in Hawaii, you were getting the best of medical care.

A day later, on the third day, you died with all of us around your bed. I said, "We love you," which you could no longer hear. I called your doctor who drove out to the house from Hilo to register your death. The hearse arrived. I turned my back as they took you out the door, feet first.

On the following morning, riding out to Hilo to select your casket, the sky was brilliant like those fall leaves in Jackson with streaks of sunlight bursting outward. If I looked with imagination, I could see Buddha in the center. We held a wake for you at the house so you would make your final departure from home. Your casket was set in front of our family shrine. Your friend Togo-san sat near your casket throughout the night and never left until the sun came up.

A week before you died, you told Okaasan that all the Buddhist priests from your childhood up to the present were all sitting together in a circle, on the floor, singing the Buddhist sutras. "Aren't you lucky," Okaasan said, "that they are all here for you. How gratifying."

Before returning to Michigan, Okaasan told me what you said about your five children. About me, you said, "You don't need to worry about that one. That one will fall many times and will always pick herself up."

You were fifty-nine. When you died, I grieved for the child that you were, not for the honest and dignified life you had lived. You often said you were not a smart man because your mother had hit you on your head too many times when you were a child and you had to stop your education at third grade to help raise your siblings. That image of you running bare-footed over five miles of unpaved road to the village store for a gallon of shoyu or five pounds of sugar remains.

I have outlived you by many years. Sometimes I still have dreams of the morning when I called the doctor. I'm never able to get through. The dial tone is always on. I cannot make that final call. Your words became part of my being and I'm still picking myself up, unafraid. The door still needs to be fixed. My telephone call still won't go through.

Breaking the Ice

The cashier at See's Candies in Sacramento cracked the frozen silence. I choose silence when confronted with blind prejudice of any kind. Or I escape into the kitchen. As I stood in line, courage emerged from nowhere to break the silence. That cashier transported me to a cold December day in Michigan when an old farmer took me ice fishing.

I sat drifting that day, watching bluegill and bass swim beneath the frozen lake. It felt right, my farmer friend and me, here on the frozen lake in that cozy little shack. It was like living inside a Robert Frost poem, a place that didn't need my voice or my words. I sat entranced, seeing only glimpses of fish, their tails and heads darting beneath a hole, too small to reveal their whole bodies.

"Hey, Vern," I said, "look at all those fish. It's magic that we're sitting here on ice and all that life is going on underneath. Do you think our lives are like this? We live on the surface and never really know what goes on with people. Maybe we need to crack a little ice now and then." Vern didn't reply. He just continued fishing. I wondered if he heard me. After a while he finally said, "Well, if you want to crack ice, you'd better know how to swim." Swimming was something I had not learned to do, at least not when it came to breaking silence to right some wrong.

Once on Maui, a friend invited me to her friend's home for dessert. The moment I entered the living room, I knew they didn't expect someone wearing my face. They were all white and I was totally ignored. A maid went in and out of the kitchen serving coffee and dessert. I said to myself, "Okay, you think I belong in the kitchen with your maid," so I went into the kitchen, sat at the table and chatted with the maid. She was from Sweden and she knew we both belonged in the kitchen. No one in the living room seemed to notice my absence. My friend's husband was the only one aware of what was happening. He left but didn't offer to take me with him. Did he have his own silence and was afraid to come to my rescue?

I had retreated into that kitchen too many times. Until See's Candies.

At a writers' club meeting, I sensed similar racism from a member. We were in line to sign the attendance sheet when he made some reference to my race and something about my being slow signing the sheet. I eventually stopped attending meetings.

A wise principal once told me I was a coward. I was the vice president of a teachers' sorority in Hawaii. When I visited the home office in Kansas, the minute I entered, I observed, "Good grief, the walls are pure white." I learned that African American teachers were not accepted to the sorority at that time. During conversation with the staff the word "nigger" was used and I cringed at the thought of how easily "Asians" could be boiled in the same pot. I returned home and quit the sorority. The principal said, "Quitting is a coward's way, why don't you stay and make changes?" He was right, but in those days it was easier for me to quit.

Where racism hangs out, you can bet gender bias isn't far away. I always knew I was fighting in a man's world and if I forgot for a moment, there were plenty of reminders along the way. After giving the main address at a conference in Los Angeles, I was invited to sell and sign my books. A man in a three-piece suit came to the table and asked, "Did your husband write these books?" I looked at him and was too much the coward to say, "No, I'm the author. Do you think I'd be sitting here on my hemorrhoids promoting a husband's books?"

I also chose silence when a tourist in Hawaii paused at my book signing table, a half-dried lei still hanging around his neck over his loud aloha shirt. "Did you write these books? You wrote these books?" He shouted to his wife, "Martha, come on over. This woman wrote these books. Can you believe it? Come on over and see this." "Idiot," I didn't say, "Where on earth do you call home?"

There's a special place, called hell, for Japanese women poets in Hawaii. In my thirties, after my first book of poems was published, a Japanese district court judge was heard predicting, "No Japanese man will ever date her. She stepped into the haole world by publishing poetry." That judge proved to be right. A few weeks later I was introduced to an eligible Japanese American man. All he had to say to me was, "I don't read poetry." Then he turned and left. When a mayor of the same race said the same to me as that bachelor, I did get up the courage to retaliate. I sent him a copy of my book.

A Buddhist Zen minister was no exception to this disease of blind prejudice. After reading one of my poems on roses, he commented, "Roses have thorns and they seem to be your favorite flower; you are too harsh a human being." He advised me to leave my work and life in Hawaii and go to Japan to a monastery to "learn a little humility" by carrying an empty rice bowl in the streets. I bowed respectfully and left, hiding the tears welling up at being so cruelly judged by someone I had turned to for wisdom and compassion. That evening, a woman from the Zen center called to say I shouldn't have asked questions, only men are allowed to be heard.

I engaged a therapist to help me crack through that ice of insult and silence that surrounded me. I was working at the state office of the Department of Education when one of the administrators cautioned me, "No matter what you write, it will never be good enough and won't be accepted without edits and demands for revisions." The therapist tried to help me be more assertive and vocal when confronted with these types of power plays.

In one role-play, the therapist asked me to act angry and tell him off. I did. He looked at me and said, "Do you know you were smiling the whole time? You're still trying to be that nice Japanese girl."

At See's Candies that day, there were two men in line waiting for the cashier. When my turn came the cashier frowned and asked in suspicious tone, "Did you cut in line?" I turned around. There was no one behind me. I knew my face was my only crime. My old self would have said nothing and left.

My newer self responded, "Did you ask these two men in front of me if they cut in line? Why are you asking this only to me when there is no one behind me?"

She didn't say anything, so I persisted, "No, I need to know why you asked if I had cut in line." There was complete silence in the shop as shoppers all turned toward us. The cashier mumbled, "I saw people looking at you."

"So, "I continued, "if someone stares at me, it means I've cut in line?"

She didn't answer, and I paid for my purchase. Before leaving I looked at the cashier, who kept her eyes averted from mine, and I announced so all could hear, "I am so sorry I caused such problems for you."

I left with my purchase, feeling empowered. Bravo! Yes! That woman had given me the ice pick to chip away the ice and go fishing for the words that were just waiting to jump into my skillet. Whoa! Did they sizzle! My only regret is not sending this See's Candies encounter to their home office, for surely I would have received cases of my favorite See's Scotchmallow. Or maybe not.

I wrote and posted this poem on Facebook and on my blog to totally release that day at See's Candies. A male reader responded, "Thank you, I will spit out 'nigger' from now on. I've been keeping them all inside too long."

"Eh Jap!"

It claws my spine,
Tearing skin.
It enters my body
To devour who I am.
I spit it out! Bullseye!
So what do you do
With "Eh Jap!"
On your face?

A Stranger at Thanksgiving

I shall be telling this with a sigh
Somewhere ages and ages hence:
Two roads diverged in a wood, and I—

—"The Road Not Taken," by Robert Frost

Do you ever wonder about all those "other roads" you have not traveled? There are two I remember now, among many.

Early in my teaching career, I was writing curriculum for the State of Hawaii, Department of Education, when a private firm contracted me to write a script to be produced for high school students. This was followed by an offer for a full-time job as a script writer.

A script writer versus a curriculum writer/teacher. It was clear which would get me to Hollywood. I began leaning toward the more glamorous, the more artsy, the less conservative. After weeks of living on a pendulum, I swung back to my mother's voice: "Stay with the State. It's more secure and when you retire, you're going to need that state retirement and health insurance."

Another road diverged soon after. During those years as a classroom teacher, I spent my summers away from Hawaii, hoping to return to the students refreshed with new experiences and ideas in the fall. One summer I sent a letter to a huge ranch in Nebraska, offering to be their summer cook. I pictured all the ranch hands around the rectangular wooden table, asking for seconds of steaks broiled in teriyaki sauce. I'd seen enough John Wayne westerns to know some of those ranch hands were the Marlboro man.

"My men would enjoy teriyaki steaks for a change," the rancher called with a chuckle, and offered me the job. At the last minute, I turned into a chicken.

I wonder where I would be today had I taken one of those roads less traveled. Having a drink with Jim and Steve, as in Cameron and Spielberg? Hosting my own *Cowboy Cuisine* TV show? How did I turn cowardly? Or was it something deeper than a lack of courage?

Abunai... abunai... "Dangerous" in Japanese. Somewhere in my memory is my mother's voice echoing, "Abunai." Was it a mother's strong instinct to protect her children or was it her *nisei* upbringing, having been raised by a single *issei* mother and a nisei brother? Her arranged marriage at age nineteen clipped both wings so she could become a housewife. With abunai came that deep sense of responsibility, stability, loyalty and honor to family and the workplace.

And yet ... and yet ... there was also my mother's voice that said, "Go—where I could not go." So, conflict was part of my *sansei* history: abunai, go ... but perhaps with just one wing? I don't want to be another Icarus.

I didn't regret being the woman I had become, because within me lived a passion stronger than my Japanese heritage, a passion that gave me perhaps one-and-a-half wings to fly ... until I saw a stranger who gave me two full wings.

He was sitting at a table not far from me and my friends one Thanksgiving evening in a Las Vegas restaurant. He was dressed in a three-piece suit, dining alone. It was almost as though I sat across from him as I observed him enjoying his entrée with glasses of white wine, followed by dessert and coffee. He had no book or newspaper to keep him company. He gave me, without knowing, permission to be freer and more independent. I was in my forties by then, and still restrained by cultural norms that dictated how a woman ought to live. "I'm going to be him" became my new mantra.

After leaving Las Vegas, my first act of freedom was to enter a theater alone. It took many weeks to become that independent woman who needed no date or any companion to go see a movie. Damn that, "Oh, look at that poor woman, alone in a theater" reaction.

Yet, I kept postponing my theater venture. "I'll go next week," I said, and next week came and went. This continued on for almost a month until finally I took in a matinee. I sat behind a family, thinking perhaps I would be safer there, and observed many single men and women sitting alone. What? No one took any notice of me! How silly I felt that it had taken me over a month of anxious planning to get there. Next I attended a movie on a weeknight, more courageous and confident. I sat in the middle of the theater, away from others, munching overly salted popcorn. Then for my finale, I entered a theater alone on a Saturday night. I don't recall any of the movies.

All right, Mr. Stranger from Las Vegas, next will be dinner in a fine restaurant. I can do this. I was scheduled to give a lecture at a conference in Los Angeles, and a hotel reservation was provided. Do I ask for room service, or do I dress and join others in the elegant dining room? I took my cue from the Stranger and entered the dining room. The bartender must have been curious about this woman sitting alone. He came over to chat and suggested I join him at his bar. Holding my head high, I gently rejected his offer. I had my entrée, a glass of wine and dessert and coffee without a book or notebook to give the appearance I was there for a business meeting. It was easily done, but in a strange city I had anonymity. Could I do this in Honolulu where everyone knew my name? Well, even two can become everyone in your hometown.

I walked into a downtown Woolworth's by myself and sat at their counter and chatted with the waitress, checking off another great milestone. I began with lunches, then dinners, and knew I had reached my goal when I was invited to give a poetry reading at a luncheon sponsored by the Small Business Women's group. The hostess introduced me by saying, "Frances is the only woman I know who dines alone by candlelight, even at home." I didn't realize I'd gained real freedom by dining alone at home by candlelight. I wondered if my Stranger from Las Vegas also dined alone at home by candlelight. He is still with me as I travel solo to strange cities, giving me the courage to be comfortable on my own. I wish I could thank him, for he gave me not only independence but also, indirectly, the ability to speak with strangers as well, something I hadn't done that night in Vegas.

It was at Volcano House on the Big Island of Hawaii. I had a room there and had gone down to the dining room for dinner. Two tables away, I observed a nicely dressed elderly woman sitting alone. She started her dinner with *ohelo* pie which is endemic to the volcano area. After the plate was taken away, the waiter brought her a bowl of soup, followed by her entrée. I was intrigued and walked over to tell her, "I'm so impressed with you. You had dessert first for your dinner. Now that is true freedom."

She asked me to sit and told me this story. "All my childhood, I was forced to eat my vegetables before I could have dessert. I missed out on a lot of desserts because I hated those steamed vegetables. Now that I'm older, I make my own rules. I always have dessert first. You ought to try it sometimes."

Have I ever dined alone at Thanksgiving or Christmas? Not yet, but I will, should I find myself alone during these two holidays. If that Stranger can do it, why can't I? And I will definitely begin with dessert. And should Hollywood call, I will certainly say yes.

Becoming Sansei

My fingers bleed
Untying obi knots.
Layer after layer of kimono silk
Now free to flow, cling,
Wet against skin.
Won't the sun ever rise?
Slowly, slowly, layer after layer
Unwraps itself and gently falls ...
Silk clouds at my feet.
I stand, naked, to become.
I kneel and lift cherry blossoms,
A chrysanthemum,
Breathe in the aroma of green tea,
Under the rising sun.
And I become.

Last Star Laughing

Norma, a dear friend, once said, "I've never met anyone who died so many times." If I were my own therapist, I might link it back to when I was five. Pearl Harbor was bombed and the only sense I could make of the world after that was there was danger all around me and I could die. There were sirens alerting us to run to air raid shelters, soldiers camped right across from Kapoho School with their tanks and guns in plain view, truckloads of soldiers following us home and the necessity of timing our walks home from school to avoid possible air attacks from the Japanese. Death was always close by in those days. Friends and relatives killed in the war, blackout curtains and civil defense exercises. The Korean war followed me through high school, to keep death and dying close. Many of my poems written in high school were about the Korean War.

I wanted to live. I promised to be good so I could go to seventh grade, so I wouldn't miss out on wearing shoes to school for the first time. From seventh grade on, there was a growing list of things I had to achieve before I died. Finally, I reached an age when every future is uncertain and to be glad I survived the past and made it to the present.

I wanted to live. Yet, every time I saw a doctor, I imagined I had some fatal disease. When my first book of poetry was published, I was certain I would have a short life because the gods were rushing my childhood dream of becoming a writer. I would probably die at age forty. Each day challenged me to live on mountain tops or in the deepest oceans of my imagination. Writing poetry and stories was my way to push back against death, and I kept on pushing, over and over.

I wish now I had listened more to the people assuring me that I would experience only one death, and to just keep pushing: the rest of it was life.

I scribbled in my journal:

> Something is being orchestrated here and I'm not sure whether I'm to take hold of a baton or to just sit quietly in the corner and listen and listen to the music.

> I received a message from Scott Stone last week—"Send my love to Frances." His doctor gave him two months to live.

> He referred to his cancer as a "nuisance" and how it hasn't stopped him from writing and isn't it enjoyable to be able to write, even if we don't sell. He thanked me for the bottle of rum. I find it so difficult to discuss his cancer and dying so my communications have been sparse.

> I revisited my poems written when the thought of death was passing through my mind. Poems I'd written during my most fearful times of not living to a respectably old

age. I wrote Scott, yes, thank God we can still write, even if it's only death we're writing about.

Scott and I have never seen each other. He, a journalist, interviewed me over the phone for my inclusion in the book Outstanding Women of the 20th Century. *I also read one of his books and sent him my personal critique. We made plans to meet in Hawaii for rum and Coke but it never came to.*

Rum and Coke became our instant connection. In his book he referred to rum and Coke as the drink after WWII which no one today would know about. "Wrong!" I said, "I drank rum and Coke in college." Scott died without our rum and Coke, but I toast him with one now and then, and hope someone will do the same for me when it's my time.

My good friend Fay was dying in Kansas. Her husband, Bill, emailed me daily, comforting me with, "Frances, don't be sad. She's dying and this is part of living."

My friend Norma died of cancer, too. I cried over the phone about it, and she comforted me. "Feel my arms around you. You're going to be all right." "I don't want you to die," I sobbed. She asked me to write her some poems instead of being sad, so I did. It helped. How is it the sick and dying can become the strong ones who comfort the weak? We never talked about her illness on those days I visited her in San Diego. Only in the letters we exchanged during that time.

I always thought death meant *Rage, rage against the dying of the light*. What my dear friends were teaching me, the ones who actually faced that moment, was that accepting death was not the same as giving up life. My poems from the time reveal that I still had a long way to go.

During each period of "dying," it was poetry that helped me make sense of what was happening. Here are five poems "raging against the dying of the light."

Cancer?

"We need a biopsy,"
He matter-of-factly tells me,
Looking at me straight in the eyes.
"It may be cancer."
Cancer? How dare you say
Cancer.
Why not something
Vague and unclear like
"Unforeseen cell growth" or
Why not even,
"There's probably nothing wrong with you
But we'll take tests anyway."
Damn you! How dare you say
Cancer
And look at me
Straight in the eyes.
Lie to me, you bastard!
Suddenly I realize

He is waiting for me to speak.
I say nothing.
I only look him straight
In the eyes.
Cancer?

Prognosis: Cancer

Like a lightning bolt,
He sizzles d-e-a-t-h
Upon my back.
Why didn't you lie
When I said
I wanted the truth?
The Artist
In his Gallery
Pinpoints
My imperfection
On the screen.
Are you sure
You know my name?
A statistician
Drops a number
Into my womb.
If I smile
Will he wake me
From this lie?
The Arctic Wind
It chills and freezes.
Fire to Ice. Fire to Ice

I promise to be good.
I don't want to die.
Ice.

Surgery

As white knights
Gather around me
I think sadly:
If I should die
No one in this immaculate room
Will shed half a tear
My heart and lungs
And my gall bladder
Anonymous
As a faceless stranger
In a crowd.
These white knights
Circling, lying.
They cannot hear
My rage against
This anonymity.
I did rage
Against this black night.
Dylan Thomas.

Where Are the Pretty Thoughts?

"This will sting you a little,"
The anesthesiologist quietly, soothingly says.
"This will make you somewhat drowsy."

Slowly lose control
Of my feelings and thoughts as I begin to drift.
How many times a day has he said this to patients
Who tensely hear it for the first time?
I open my eyes, heavy with sleep
And see the ceiling wave above me.
Then the thought of dying
Enters my mind.
"I may never come out of this,"
I panic, and begin to find
Breathing a not-so-natural process.
My insides begin to tremble.
The trembling slowly crawls outside my skin
To my arms and inner thighs.
God, I'm so terribly alone and frightened.
Who can help me?
No one can, not even a mother, a lover, or a best
    friend.
Think pretty thoughts, I tell myself.
Pretty thoughts. What are pretty thoughts?
Meadows with brooks? Birds? Flowers?
Christmas. Yes, Christmas.
The trees go on sale tomorrow.
My students, perhaps. Let me see their faces.
What are pretty thoughts
When the fear of dying becomes the only reality?
The tightening gets tighter.
Tomorrow, I'll think of this time tomorrow.
I'll be in my own bed, laughing over this.
I'll be sharing this idiotic fear with someone.

Tomorrow, but all the tomorrows do not help.
The chilling and trembling continue.
Can I ask them to stop? Yes, I'll ask them to stop.
More intravenous anesthesia.
I slowly lose consciousness,
Hearing the muffled voices of
The White Knights around the
Cold, rectangular table.
Where are my pretty thoughts?
What can they be?
I don't want to die.

The Verdict

"There's no malignancy."
He looks me straight
In the eyes.
I say nothing.
I look him
Straight in his eyes
And I smile and smile
And smile.

How do you talk to people who are dying? Once, when I thought I had cancer, my young nephew asked me directly, "Are you going to die?" We talked about it. With a child, I'm able to put up an adult front and discuss almost any topic if it might bring with it some understanding.

I didn't really get it at all until my friend Gwen Lee put it all together for me and held it up so even I could see it. I was waiting for a medical test and wondered if it would reveal cancer. "I might die," I blurted out to Gwen.

"Can I have your Ming's pearl bracelet?" was all that Gwen said. And that made it all right. Very all right. We laughed and fantasized about my dying scene. The whole thing was settled. I knew then that it has to be done with humor.

During the late seventies, a surgeon did for me what Gwen had done. I was searching for the right physician to cure my stomach pain. The first doctor on Oahu said I had ulcers, put me on a strict diet and told me to enjoy my Christmas because most Japanese die from stomach cancer. I walked out and never returned. I returned home to our family doctor in Hilo, and he chose denial and diagnosed, "There's nothing wrong with you." Back to Oahu, I saw another doctor who diagnosed a tumor in my gall bladder. He knew of my fear and tried various medications and waited for me to say, "I'm ready for surgery."

In the meantime, my yoga teacher professed to cure cancer, put me on a diet of lemon juice and cayenne pepper. "This will clear out your tumor," she said, until one night I heard the panic in her voice when I told her I was bleeding profusely from my rectum.

I returned to the doctor, who said, "I thought you were more intelligent than this." After more X-rays, he called in the surgeon. The surgeon walked in, looked at the X-rays and said my gall bladder definitely showed tumors and needed to be removed. He looked at my face and casually said, "Oh, we'll just take your gall bladder out and feed it to the cat." His comment gave me such relief; he made me feel, as we say in Hawaii, "it ain't no big thing." On the night of the surgery, I wrote the following poem and left it at my bedside, which was found by the surgeon while I was asleep. He, a poet/surgeon, understood and we would later share poems and a friendship.

On the Eve of Surgery

An unfriendly morn
Awaits my awakening.
Whatever his face
I'll greet him with mine.
If his breath
Should suck mine dry,
I'll take his hand
Into mine,
And gently leave
By morning's light.

If there is an art to dying, I hope to go as Art Buchwald did, the political humorist who brought laughter to his bedside. As life would have it, I'm given dry runs, so to speak. I once told a dying friend, "Since you're going before me, can you wait for me with a mink-lined recliner when it's my turn? Real mink." Our laughter filled the room.

Don, a member of my poetry writing support group,

questioned which would be the best way to die, cancer or dementia. I recalled the number of times I'd speculated about my illness and death. It is easy to do when dying is not even close to reality and we're invincibly healthy.

Yes, I do have my choice if given one, I told Don. I don't want to die without notice. Hear that, Death? Give me a few months so I can say good-bye to all my friends and family members and time to burn my journals and my shoe box of old love letters. And time to tell a good joke. Hey, did I tell you about the poet who walked into a bar? But just in case, my partner Red and I have already said our good-byes over dinner, should we be apart when the time comes. None of those Hollywood scenes where the most important words are said at the deathbed.

> In one of those stars
> I shall be living.
> In one of them I shall be laughing.
> And so it will be as if all the stars were laughing,
> When you look at the sky at night.
> And when your sorrow is comforted (time soothes
>   all sorrows)
> You will be content that you have known me.
> You will always be my friend ...
> I shall not leave you.
>
> —*The Little Prince*, Antoine de Saint-Exupéry

Last Call

It's true, Mrs. Maeda, the midwife of Kapoho, brought me and my tiny baby feet into the world, just as she had done for so many of us village urchins, the ones I grew up with, the boys who would call me Stew Bones for being skinny and flat-chested in high school, or the ones who stood by me as I struggled to talk like the haoles, which I thought would fulfill my dreams beyond the outhouses of Kapoho. "You're going college," they'd say.

It wasn't Mrs. Maeda's magical hands or the kids around me who got me born and breathing in the world with its airs of insults and exaltations. I took my first real breath in first grade. It was the day the teacher read us poetry and I saw how words could create magical images in my head. "I can do that!" I thought. "I can make images of flowers dancing in the wind like these words do! I'm going to be a writer!" I thought. And I meant it.

That's what got me started on all this. Imagination's winding road, I found out, had just as many pitfalls and dead ends as all the other "more traveled" roads. There were the years I wanted to become an actress in Hollywood after watching the parade of cars driving by the cane field to an on-location filming of *Bird of Paradise* while I waved to Louis Jourdan, Jeff Chandler and Debra Paget, who I knew were in one of those cars.

During the war, my imagination had me stepping on green bugs to weaken the enemy and to end the way Japanese Americans were being treated, because my sister had told me they were "Japanese bugs."

Now, when I see the same sun that first lit up my life approach its other great horizon, I feel beckoned off the track of writing and poetry. Writing and poetry were inside of me. I discovered them at a very early age. But these other lessons on being in the world as I would want it to be came through the examples of others.

"The best kind of mechanic," I said to the graduating class at Pahoa School in my commencement address, "is a poet mechanic. The best scientist is a poet scientist. The best bus driver is a poet bus driver. The best doctor, a poet doctor. When you become a poet, you begin your profession by being a human first, though not necessarily a person who writes poetry."

There have been many such poets in my life who taught me to live poetically first. When I took my first driver's test in a fellow teacher's standard-shift car along the winding country road in Laupahoehoe, the officer said, "Stop the car. You're driving in neutral down this road which is very dangerous. Do not use your clutch, use your brake to slow down." At the end of the test drive he said, "I know you made many mistakes because you're nervous. You'll have confidence after you get your license." I got my license, and I didn't even have his child in my class.

There was that policeman in Jackson, Michigan, who accompanied me on my driver's road test. While struggling to parallel park between two cars on a snowy, wintry day, he quietly said, "I don't think you're going to make it ... why don't you park between those two cars over there ... there's more space between those two," and I did. He approved my road test and said, "Aloha, I hope you enjoy Michigan."

I first became aware of such poets at Pahoa High School ... a village hick in classrooms lit with her first electric lights. We may not have had the most qualified teachers—a coach who had to teach algebra, or the English teacher teaching the Spanish class. I needed two foreign language as well as Algebra I and II credits to apply to the University of Hawaii, but our curriculum offered only one class of each. For many teachers, our school was their first teaching positions out of teachers' college; luckily, they were poets first, too. Somehow, they knew of my drive to attend college. So after Algebra I, the coach gave me an Algebra II book and said, "Sit in the back of my Algebra I class and study this textbook."

The English teacher did the same: Sit in the back of my Spanish I class and study this Spanish II text. I got the credits I needed.

Meanwhile, my social studies teacher gave me history books to study to prepare for the entrance exams to the university.

Students from Kapoho took the early bus to Pahoa High School and we sat shivering in the dark hallways waiting for the day to begin. During my senior year, three teachers from the teachers' cottages invited me to their cottage every morning. They left the door unlocked so I could enter without waking them. I went into the kitchen and made coffee and toast. We all had breakfast together, with a male teacher from another cottage. They didn't write poetry, they lived it.

I never forgot the teacher who took me to the hair salon in Hilo for a permanent so I could look my best and attend the prom with pride and confidence. The boys teased, "Hey, you got electrocuted. Nice curls!"

Poet teachers also appeared at the University of Hawaii, Hilo. Overnight trips to dig for Hawaiian artifacts on old burial grounds was a course requirement in Anthropology. I told the professor that I was working as a live-in maid for room and board and would not be able to take overnight trips. The professor said, "These artifacts need to be carefully brushed and cleaned, why don't you come to the lab during your free time to do this. Take them home, if you wish. That will meet your requirement for the course."

Throughout my freshman year in college, my sixth-grade teacher, who had me suspended from school after she found a nasty note I had scribbled about her, kept in touch and corrected my poorly crafted letters and returned them to me, to teach me perhaps what she had failed to do or what I had failed to learn.

I was fortunate to have others along the way to show me the meaning of kindness and generosity. On Oahu, my primary care physician invited me to help prepare and deliver a full Thanksgiving dinner to all his shut-in patients. We worked all morning in his kitchen and it was one of my best Thanksgivings, seeing the joy on his patients' faces who were in hospital beds in their living rooms or who came to the door in wheelchairs or walkers.

Bearers of this humanity even appeared in malls and hardware stores. My shopping cart began to squeak with the most irritating metal against metal sound, so high up the scale that mice in ceilings would have fallen dead. Shoppers began to frown at me. The wheels on my car turned sideways. I continued my slow walk toward the cashiers who were aisles away. More stares. Then one man said aloud, "I like that sound!" Everyone froze and looked at him. I saw his smiling face and wanted to hug him for knowing what was happening and the exact right thing to do. His smile gave me the courage to say aloud so all could hear, "And I love irritating people!" The only person who laughed was that male shopper. We exchanged smiles and a nod, and I squeaked my way toward the cashier.

I have watched enough *NCIS* to know that a camera can pinpoint the exact time to the minute when a crime has been committed and a blurred face can be recognized through our advanced technology. I should have known this as I worked toward becoming a thief.

I walk inside the mall for an hour in the mornings before the shops open. Often, the security guards and I are the only ones in the mall. The mall is filled with beautiful plants. One of those potted plants is selling for $27 or more at nursery shops or at supermarkets. So, why can't I just snip off a cutting and start my own pot of greens? Who would miss a five-inch cutting? There are two such pots in one corner of the mall. I could easily hide one in my pocket. Each time I passed those potted plants, I stopped and said, "It wouldn't hurt anyone, just a break in that stem." Then one day a security guard, in his attempt to assure me that the mall is safe, said, "There are more than 150 cameras in the ceilings."

OMG, I thought, looking up at the ceiling, I could have been arrested for stealing. But the thought never left. Will they arrest an Asian woman, masked, who steals a six-inch stem from a plant?

One morning, I saw the gardener working with the plants. I asked to see his trash bag for any cuttings. I told him how pricey those potted plants were and that I would like some cuttings. He asked which plants did I like? Without a word he took out two potted plants, put them in a plastic bag and said, "Walk with me and show me what other plants you want." I told him those two pots were enough. "These are heavy. Let me carry these to your car." He refused the cash I offered him for his lunch. A week later, he had a potted palm tree. "Take this to your car, if Security stops you, tell them Jose gave you this."

He not only saved me from prison, but he brought unsolicited kindness into my life on those two mundane mornings. We were evidently being observed because other walkers since then have gifted me with potted plants. Jose and I exchange "Good Morning" now.

That sense of valuing others and treating everyone with respect for what was right must have come from our parents. It wasn't always clear which path to take when it came to human interactions. Writing alone couldn't tell me which way to go. Sometimes it was something my parents said about kindness and having compassion. More often it was the things they didn't say, the times they didn't scold me of my mistakes and failings. They knew about my little deceptions and my habit of breaking a few rules now and again, but decided to let me find out for myself alone what I could get away with and what crossed the line. Above all, I think they had faith I would learn, in time, that kindness and being thankful for what was given to me were the only roads that would serve me no matter where I went or what I did. And they in turn, will return to me.

Songs of Kapoho

I will be called a racist and tarnish the memory of Kapoho unless I appear before you as an anthropologist so here I am, the Margaret Mead of Kapoho.

Kapoho was a conglomerate of many cultures and produced children who grew up accepting their multi-cultural heritage. I can recall only one glitch along the way, which developed after December 7, 1941. Following the Pearl Harbor attack, a new three-letter word entered our lexicon, "Jap." It was introduced to the village from films and news reports. But that word was short-lived in Kapoho.

Our diet demonstrated the interrelatedness of these cultures. Children followed a Korean bachelor named Kim around the village and imitated him. In his pocket he carried an endless supply of garlic, on which he snacked, so we filled our pockets with garlic and ate along with him. He didn't say a word, nor did he chase us away; he just let us be. I found the garlic too strong, so I often sneaked into our kitchen and stuffed a handful of dried shrimps into my pocket to lessen the garlic taste. Dried shrimps were constant in our meals as were Spam and Vienna sausage.

In one part of the village stood a collection of small private homes for plantation workers from the Philippines who arrived without their mates, hoping to return one day. Eventually, they sent for their women. They added *bagoóng*, pickled raw intestines of fish to our bowls of steamed rice.

There was one mysterious German woman married to a Filipino who lived at the edge of our baseball field. I visited her often to watch her weave beautiful mats and lamp shades from *lauhala* leaves. We never talked, so I didn't know how she had found her way to remote Kapoho. She fed me strudel.

The lighthouse keeper was a Portuguese man whose family introduced us to Portuguese bread. And of course there were the Hawaiians who lived near the ocean and the Japanese scattered around the village, who added their *poi*, fresh *opihi*, *sashimi* and *sushi* to our feast.

It was at school that the children from different cultures became one. Although there were no African Americans in Kapoho, we knew of their existence through our school books. Kapoho School, with its limited supply of educational materials, had no library, but our teachers read us books on the history of Black culture. I grew up listening to and reading books about slavery. Images of families being separated on the auction blocks never left my head. Our only music curriculum was based on Stephen Foster's green song books, so we sang spirituals and ballads from the pre-Civil War South.

What might be seen as deprivation today was rich soil for us, teaching us about compassion and dignity and our capacity for cruelty as revealed in history. Our school lunches were haole with spaghetti, canned peas and Spanish rice. A teacher told me years later how they spent their small paychecks on olives and cheese, food we had never tasted. Olives became "holiday food."

In a village of such cultural diversity, it was inevitable that we ate songs, too. The children became poets, masters of jingles and rhyming.

Of the Filipinos, we sang:

> O Philippine, My Philippine,
> Every time fight but no can win.
> He run and run but no can win.
> My people eat potato leaf.
> O Philippine, My Philippine,
> Every time fight but no can win.

Of the Chinese, we recited:

> Chin chin China man
> Sitting on a fence
> Trying to make a dollar
> Out of fifteen cents.

We saw the Portuguese as haoles, and being told that haoles take a bath only on Saturdays, our jingle was:

> Pologee Pologee
> No mo wash wash,

One weekee, two weekee
No mo wash wash.

There were no jingles about the Hawaiians. We didn't dare say or sing anything about the Hawaiians because we lived in fear of their God, Kahuna. But we loved their *kalua* pig and *lomilomi* salmon.

We respected the land and its original people, just as we respected the fire goddess Pele. I had a personal link to Kahuna when a fourth-grader managed to have me do her math homework for two years, threatening to put Kahuna on me if I didn't. We sang and danced many Hawaiian songs in class.

Were there any jingles about the Japanese? I'm sure there were but they were never sung to our faces, as we never sang ours within earshot of the people in our songs.

Our creativity wasn't only ethnically based, animals got their share of our harmless ignorance and here's a song showing off our rhyming skills.

Oh, the monkey wrapped his tail
Around the flagpole
To see his asshole.

We would have been good subjects for a PhD dissertation on linguistics.

Our May Day program was an annual event where all students wore their native costumes and danced their ethnic dances. It was the *kimono* for me, the bamboo dance for the Filipinos, the hula dancers in grass skirts for the Hawaiians, the Maypole dance for the haoles.

Now, if I were truly an anthropologist, I would be fascinated by the children of Kapoho. Here was a village in remote Hawaii, with no electricity or indoor plumbing. Children ran around the village undisciplined because their parents were too busy making a living. Our bare feet and home-made clothing made us look like models for ads on Care Packages. There was nothing to do but create games and songs to entertain ourselves. We snacked on sweet sugar cane and guavas and, if they were as skilled in culinary arts as I was, they'd run into their kitchen to grab some dried shrimps and garlic cloves to become Korean.

We sang or recited our songs and poetry without truly understanding about race or insults. They were simply songs and poetry. In spite of pidgin and teachers' fruitless efforts to teach us to speak English like haoles, some of us managed to become poets. What more can you ask from children who, during their summer months, got up from futons spread out on wooden floors, ate last night's left-over dinners for breakfast, ran outside to play, returned to eat more leftovers, ran out to play with their homemade toys, kites made with bamboo and newspaper, sing their songs and returned for dinner by sundown.

There was a protective shield around the children of Kapoho because they were as free as ocean waves. We swam in the ocean unsupervised, climbed trees, slid down hills on cardboard boxes, walked like trapeze artists on mango branches spanning dangerous cliffs below and ate things that we found in the wild.

Bruises or cuts were treated by chewing the soft guava-tree leaves and placing them on our wounds. I once jumped on an empty Vienna sausage can. In the round wound was what I thought were tiny intestines shown beneath the skin. I covered it with a wrapping and never told. Perhaps the water from storage tanks that often contained dead cats or birds built up antibodies in our young bodies? I'm still here.

In this microcosm of a multi-rainbow society, the whole village was a single trusted group, tended by first-generation immigrants. I never gave it much thought until I was in my twenties, when a few city friends told me I trusted people too easily. They were more cautious and advised me not to be so open. Once I let others in, they said, I wouldn't be able to remove them. Obviously, these friends didn't grow up in Kapoho.

Back to Kapoho, there was another shield of protection provided from the adults. They kept an eye on their village children to see that no harm came to them, whether they were Filipinos, Koreans, Hawaiians, Japanese, Portuguese or even haoles from the plantation manager's house, made no difference.

If I had left my sweater or slippers outside somewhere, they were returned to our porch by morning. There were no policemen called in for petty crimes or thefts. Doors were unlocked and I sat in many village kitchens, usually at dinner preparation time, so I could taste their different ethnic foods, like pig-feet soup in the kitchen of an Okinawan family.

During World War II, the "soldier babies," as they were called after the soldiers left our village, were accepted as our own and silence ruled.

In Hilo, years after we had fled the lava flow that destroyed most of Kapoho, a Filipino man approached to ask, "Are you Sadame-san's daughter?"

Was he one of the villagers who had come to our house every New Year's Eve to sing, "Happy New Year, Sadame-san," with the honorific "san" attached to his name? I couldn't place him.

Maybe he was one of the villagers who had kept an eye on me even if he heard me sing our Filipino jingle. Or who had accepted us as innocent kids and let us be, knowing we would grow up to be decent human beings? We chatted for a while in broken pidgin. A friend from Hilo asked, "Who was that?" She could not have understood the warmth I felt so I merely said, "Oh, he's from Kapoho."

This protective shield around the children grew into respect after the publication of my books about Kapoho. Instead of chastising me for exposing Kapoho to the public, they came with gratitude. My two Kapoho memoirs could not disguise who they were, not even with the name changes. They all knew the two families whose sons and father were sent to the leper colony on Molokai. There was only one family who had lost their five-year-old to a tonsillectomy gone wrong and only one plantation doctor whom we had called Horse Doctor.

During book tours in Hawaii and Los Angeles, villagers who had left Kapoho after the first eruption in 1955, all appeared. "We are the Okuda sisters," "I'm the Shimizu son." No one questioned, "Was that our family?" or commented, "I think I know who that Honda woman was." Instead I heard whisperings as they stood in line with their books to be signed, "Imagine, someone from Kapoho wrote a book about us. She preserved Kapoho for us. We are so lucky." The "Horse Doctor's" daughter thanked me for the Kapoho books because some of her memories of those times were fading. They made me feel I had taken some of their dreams along with me to be fulfilled when we evacuated and left Kapoho for good.

The old village is buried in lava today after the goddess Pele's flow in 2018. Someday, another Kapoho will rise like a phoenix. A village once again, where every child is surrounded by a protective shield, regardless of race, gender or ethnicity, and is given the freedom to explore and become. Where doors have no keys and children learn trust. That is the Kapoho way, to see the good in each other.

I had to find a way to escape because Kapoho was no New York City, Paris or Hollywood. Little did I know then, wherever I went, whatever I was to become, I would always be a child of Kapoho, which isn't such a bad thing.

Epilogue

I began with poets, and it seems only right to use poetry to bring this to a close with doors slightly ajar. There is no ending to this journey of knowing what it means to be part of humanity and to preserve our planet. To ignore one over the other would lead to catastrophic results. The following poems, written from observations and encounters, speak of our responsibility to our children. Just as the stories in this book will hopefully give you pause to remember those who made a difference in your life, may we all aspire to will this to our children. And if you do, I may give you my pearl bracelet.

Your Inheritance

This Earth you call home
Was not created by chance.
There was no magic wand
That preserved man's humanity to man.
There was no magic wand
That kept all life in oceans, air and land
Free and clean
So you could breathe, swim, drink, live
Without fear or peril.
There was no magic wand.

It was I, millions of I's
Generation after generation
Who preserved, restored, and renewed
This legacy now in your name
Stewards of the new world.

—from *What Kind of Ancestor Do You Want to Be?*

To Children of the 21st Century

How do you keep your fingers so free of dirt?
How do you come in from play without
Mud on your feet, your clothes, your cheeks?
How do you not even sweat?
Do you know how rain feels
Soaking your shirt to your skin?
The smell of sea salt in your hair
After a dip in the sea?
Have you watched a little seed
Pushing its first breath
Out of soil you've patted down
A few weeks ago?
Can you see a cardinal, a mynah,
A crow, with your eyes closed, listening
To their signature songs they sing to you
In your own back yard?
Do you know the feel of the crisp
New pages of a book, as they unfold
Plots moving faster than your impatient
Fingers can follow your eyes?
Do you live without giving eye contact?
Is the person sitting in front of you
Just the back of a head
Without a thought?

Oh Children of the 21st Century,
Why is there silence in a room filled
With family on this holiday?
How did you become so mute?
Do you know the feel of your grandpa's grip
Warm and strong in your hand?
Or the story behind that long scar
That runs the length of his arm?
Do you carry the memories
Of your grandma's smiles
When you said,
Hi Grandma. Can I help you?
Do you count clouds, lying
On soft green grass, laughing
Over silly stuff shared with a friend?
You ever cry over a child hungry
On your street, in the world?
Ever feel upset over trees being cut
For freeways and shopping malls,
Fancy sports arenas?
You do know what it means to be kind
Compassionate, giving.
Though the face in the mirror
Is not yours. Let that be your first poem.

Dear 21st Century Farmer

Each time you place a seed into your soil,
What do you think about?
Do you think of fast cash
To replace your brain
For a larger, more digitized tractor?
Insect eradication for abundant crops?
Vocabulary rested on faster, more, faster, more
Or do faces of your grandchildren, their
    grandchildren
Play among the images in your head?
The inheritors of your soil.
Each time you place a seed into your soil,
Do you get down on your back,
Look up at white clouds dancing, dancing -
Pesticides free, gathering raindrops
For Earth's purification?
Each time you place a seed into your soil,
Can you take a fistful of soil —
Taste the taste of soil
As they were before you were courted
By "Big Six" pesticide and GMO corporations —
BASF, Bayer, Dupont, Dow Chemical Co. Monsanto,
    Syngenta?
Oh, farmer of the 21st century,
Are you indignant at these questions?

Let me hear then, your "How dare you.
How dare you
Question the integrity of my soul.
How dare you
Before my grandchildren
And their future children.
I am not a farmer for sale!"

Tree

I see you.
Put that saw away.
You will not use my sisters and brothers
To fill your bank account
With Real Estate towers.
I see you.
Put that saw down.
Look up at my glory,
Home to hundreds of life
More than you can accommodate
In your blue-printed home of destruction.
See me.
Before it is too late.

Raised by Wolves with Apologies to Wolves

Are we letting wolves raise our children?

I walk inside the mall before the shops open and exchange "Good Morning" with a few elderly walkers. Twice last week, when I said, "Good Morning" to two young adults, they looked stunned and said, "Oh, okay." They reminded me of a young man who sat next to me on a flight to Hawaii.

Raised by Wolves

A young man buckles himself next to me,
Connected to wires and earbuds.
He grunts to my Hello without meeting my eyes.
Soon we are flying over the Pacific
Nary a word between our proximity.
An hour into flight, breakfast trays appear.
He leans over his mushroom cheese crepes,
Stabs his fork into one, lifts the crepe to his mouth,
Takes a bite and drops the rest of the crepe to his
    plate.
He was raised by wolves, this much I know.
He picks up a piece of cantaloupe with his fingers
Takes a bite, moves his face over his tray and drops

The size too large for a bite back to his plate.
His utensils, ignored like the napkin on his tray.
My teacher mode kicks in.
Learn by observing, child raised by wolves.
Learn by observing.
Miss Manners and Emily Post at his service
I use each silverware and my napkin, too.
Attempt again for conversation over breakfast.
"Let me guess," I begin.
No, no, I didn't ask, "Were you raised by wolves?"
Miss Manners was still around.
"You're a college student returning home for
    summer break."
He flashes his first smile. He finished his junior
    year in college,
Flying home with hopes of finding a summer job.
I drink my cup of decaf coffee, wish him well.
I was wrong, not raised by wolves, but perhaps
By fast food finger foods and his smartphone.

Address Books and Matchbook Covers

Have you ever gone through the belongings of your loved ones after they're gone?

In 2002, I found in my mother's bureau every Mother's Day card she had received from her children. Included were handwritten letters of thanks sent by her physician. These letters told me my mother had regularly dropped off orchids and papayas from the farm where she worked. I sent these letters back to the doctor and he was totally moved that my mother had saved each one. There was the handkerchief I had made for Mother's Day when I was in the fifth grade. She lost to Alzheimer's, but I found her stories in her belongings.

I wrote this poem after observing two people exchange phone numbers. They deftly added numbers to their smartphones. What will we have after electronically saved people are deleted?

Address Books and Matchbook Covers

When I am dead, my dearest,
Will you draw a Sharpie marker

Through my name, write Dead in bold caps
Or simply press Delete
To eradicate me forever?

Or will you preserve my name under K
And years from now …
On a cold wintry afternoon when friends
Have deserted you and boredom sets in,
You flip through your address book and pause at K.
Under the slow-changing day into night, my name
appears.
You say my name and soon stories appear and you
smile and even chuckle
When there was a me and a you.
Perhaps memories will take you to a shoebox
labeled FHK
In a spider-webbed corner of the garage.
You find old, faded matchbook covers. Matchbook
covers?
Yes, matchbook covers. You flip one open and see
faded numbers.
Is it a hurriedly written phone number of a
handsome stranger I once met
In a coffee shop or in a bar? Did I call that number
and did a story begin?
Should you play sleuth and call that number? He
must be long gone by now.
Are there matchbook covers in other garages?
A shoebox of mysteries keep you awake until dawn.
Ah ha … and you thought I was gone forever.

Acknowledgments

To Linda Donahue, my first editor, for her in-depth editing. I often sent rough drafts to Linda, knowing she would straighten them out, weaving out my Kapoho-style grammar.

To Red Slider, for listening to my stories and for knowing when to say, "That's a good story, write it down," followed by his editor's pen that often left me on the defensive: "This is a good outline, now fill in the details. This poem doesn't do it. Rewrite it." And for letting me "cut in line." He was editing a friend's novel when he dropped it to edit my stories.

To Gwen Lee for planting that seed that there is always another book to be written, for her patience, waiting for the pearl bracelet and for the title of this book.

To Mark Arax for creating the Araxing editor's pen when he asked, "Do you need that last sentence/paragraph?"

To Charles Pellegrino for raising the bar when he reminded me often, "Your stories must be as good as, or better than 'Mrs. Honda's Beautiful Daughter.'"

To Wayne Harada for leaving a space for a poet/writer in his "Show Biz" column even if I can't sing or dance, except "Yellow Ginger Lei."

To all who came into my life: family, friends, strangers, former students, and now you.

Last and not least, to George Engebretson of Watermark Publishing, for adding another book to my list of Watermark published books. To Dawn Sakamoto, for working behind the scenes as though I'm her only author/client. I have lived life as a writer because of you both at Watermark Publishing. Thank you beyond words for giving me that well-lived author's life.

Glossary

Bakatare: Japanese word for stupid

Haole: Caucasian in Hawaiian

Issei: first-generation Japanese immigrant

Mochi: rice cake

Moxa: Mugwort herb

Nisei: second-generation Japanese immigrant

Nishime: Japanese dish prepared with chicken and special vegetables

Sansei: third-generation Japanese immigrant

Yaito: Burning moxa on specific places on the body for a cure of certain illnesses

About the Author

The award-winning, internationally published author of eighteen books, and a former columnist for the *Hawai'i Herald*, Frances H. Kakugawa conducts poetry readings, workshops and lectures throughout the country. In her sessions for adults, Frances shares with honesty and openness the lessons learned from caregiving. Programs for hospital and elder-healthcare professionals focus on humanizing their professional skills. In her children's workshops, Frances introduces students to poetry as a way to explore and embrace their elders and other aspects of their lives. She also conducts lectures and workshops to instruct educators on how to individualize curriculum through journals and poetry.

Frances presently resides in Sacramento, Calif., and leads a monthly poetry support group for the caregivers for the Alzheimer's Association. To book Frances for a workshop, classroom visit or lecture, email her at fhk@ francesk.org or contact her online on her Facebook Page (www.facebook.com/FrancesKakugawa) or on her blog (franceskakugawa.wordpress.com).

francesk.org

www.ingramcontent.com/pod-product-compliance
Lightning Source LLC
Chambersburg PA
CBHW051524120626
46551CB00012B/1065